THE PATH TO

PRODUCTIVE CHRISTIAN LIVING

BY JERRY M PAUL

as taught by Jesus

in the

Sermon on the Mount

The Path to Productive Christian Living

TABLE OF CONTENTS

INTRODUCTION

What does the Sermon on the Mount mean to you? Does it shape who you are as a Christian? Does it effect your outlook on the world? In what way does it impact the way you live?

The Sermon on the Mount is the most challenging message I have ever heard or read. It knocks me down, lifts me up, discourages me, encourages me, corrects me, challenges me, guides me, inspires me, and makes me take a serious, in-depth look at who I am and the way I live. Reading it, teaching it, preaching it always confronts me with the reality that these instructions from the Lord Himself show me exactly how to live the Christian life; not just live it, but live it in a productive way. The result of this spiritual stimulation? The birth of this literary child named, THE PATH TO PRODUCTIVE CHRISTIAN LIVING. My prayer is that this child will be a blessing, helping you become a more productive disciple of Jesus Christ.

No message in history compares to the one Jesus Christ gave in this Sermon on the Mount. These words of our Lord have been described as the Magna Carta of the Christian life or the Christian manifesto. They are not a dissertation about a system of beliefs or religious ceremonies, but an explanation of what it means to be a true and faithful follower of Jesus.

Christ's dynamic message explodes with surprises. Sometimes the Sermon strikes us as unrealistic and impossible. Most of it conflicts with life as we commonly experience it. Often the Lord's message is intense and demanding. Yet the rewards He offers to those who follow His instruction go beyond anything this world can give.

Undoubtedly, the Sermon on the Mount has touched more lives than any other message in history. However, not all who hear this message understand or like Jesus' words. Multitudes cannot make sense of His teaching because it contradicts too many of their preconceived and much-loved ideas about life. They argue with Jesus, try to explain away His words, and reject His instruction.

Perhaps the first step in understanding the Sermon on the Mount is to realize this message is not intended to be applied to the world generally. Rather, it speaks specifically to people who are followers of Jesus…believers, kingdom people, Christ-ians. So, if you claim to be a member of God's family join with me in putting on your 'listening ears' so we can allow the Lord Jesus Christ to teach us.

According to Matthew, *"his disciples came to him. And he opened his mouth and taught them" (5:1-2),** and in that teaching Jesus introduced His disciples to a different kind of life-style. What they heard was contrary to everything they had been taught, believed, and lived most of their lives. He presented to them a brand-new perspective on every situation in life. Jesus challenged His followers, these kingdom people, to be dramatically different persons and to live dramatically different lives.

Nowhere in this message does Jesus say, "Here is what you should believe." Rather, He presents two supremely important challenges. The Lord declares, in essence, "If you wish to be my disciple you must first be this kind of person *(5:2-12),* and, secondly, you must learn to confront the issues of life this way *(5:13-7:29).*"

Through this Sermon on the Mount Jesus takes us down the path to productive Christlike living. His instruction serves as the Christian's Constitution, providing guidance for every life situation a kingdom person faces.

Clearly, the challenges Jesus described in this truly unique life and lifestyle are overwhelming. They can be met successfully in only one way...by the power of God through complete loyalty to Jesus. For that reason, the best way to hear the Sermon on the Mount is on your knees. Prepare to be humbled. Forget all you have heard or believed in the past about how to live. Come as a new disciple hearing new words about a new life...kingdom life. Listen to Jesus' message. Ponder it; digest it; live it. With the crowds who heard Him, you also will be *"astonished at his teaching" (7:28).*

*Biblical references in this style *(5:16)* are from the Sermon on the Mount (*Matthew 5, Matthew 6* or *Matthew 7).* All other Scriptural references include the Bible book name.

* * *

Matthew 5:1-2

"Seeing the crowds, he went up on the mountain, and when he sat down, his disciples came to him. And he opened his mouth and taught them, saying: . . . "

THE CHARACTER OF THE PRODUCTIVE CHRISTIAN
5:3-12

In Your Relationship With God

CHAPTER 1

5:3-12 ... Experience The Beatitudes

Many people view the Beatitudes as eight individual sayings, each containing a principle regarding the nature of one's walk with God. While there is truth in this view the Beatitudes also function as a single unit describing the character of a disciple of Jesus, a kingdom person. This character shows itself to the world through the actions described in the rest of the Sermon on the Mount. That world, looking at the character revealed through those actions, sees one who is Christlike and godly. It sees a person who duplicates the attitudes of Christ *(Philippians 2:5)* and takes on the servanthood role as demonstrated in the actions of Jesus *(Philippians 2:6),* thereby becoming an imitator of God *(Ephesians 5:1).* The world sees a child of God...a true disciple of Jesus...a kingdom person.

Each Beatitude begins with the same truth...a truly Christlike servant of God is *"blessed."* This 'blessedness' comes through an inner serenity of mind and internal joy at the core of the kingdom person's being, not at all dependent on external situations and circumstances. The disciples of Jesus enjoy the deepest blessing of God because they understand and experience the meaningful and the eternal as described in each Beatitude.

Interestingly, the blessedness promised by Jesus is a result of being, not doing. This directly challenges our natural tendency to be more concerned about the doing..."Am I doing the right thing?... Am I doing this thing right?" Jesus starts with what the kingdom person is, not what the kingdom person does. Why? Because what the person is will determine what the person does. The doing Jesus describes in the rest of the Sermon on the Mount grows naturally out of being the kind of person described in the Beatitudes. The two are coupled of necessity. It is not possible to have one without the other. The first - being - naturally and consistently produces the second - doing; the second cannot properly exist without the first.

Both individually and as a single unit these Beatitudes hold out a standard that contrasts dramatically with the world's concepts. They are the exact opposite of the generally accepted human viewpoint, as will be immediately evident in the next chapter's examination of the first Beatitude. They conflict with almost everything the world tells us about coping with life.

None of these characteristics manifests itself naturally in the human heart and mind. Therefore, the natural human mindset doubts, questions, and rebels against the truths presented in these principles of kingdom life. This rebellion ultimately produces an ongoing conflict between the one who wants to be a servant of God and the one who is a servant of the world. So Jesus addresses this antagonism in the last Beatitude...the inevitable result of the first seven Beatitudes at work in the believer's life *(5:11-12).*

Whether examining the Beatitudes singly or as a unit our conclusion is the same. They will not be be produced in us nor experienced by us as a result of human initiative alone. Only through the presence and power of God's Holy Spirit can a kingdom person be developed. Therefore, a productive walk through the Beatitudes necessitates a walk with our hand in the hand of God. That can begin only for the disciple who approaches God with poverty of spirit. To this individual Jesus, in the first Beatitude, promises *"the kingdom of heaven" (5:3).*

CHAPTER 2

5:3 ... Acknowledge Spiritual Bankruptcy

~

"Blessed are the poor in spirit, for theirs is the kingdom of heaven."

Bankrupt...beggarly...poor...destitute. Does that picture attract you? Probably not. Even though it is not attractive to people anywhere in the world Jesus opened His Sermon on the Mount declaring the road to blessedness begins by being bankrupt, beggarly, poor, destitute. However, He was not speaking about a poverty of material things. He described spiritual bankruptcy...recognizing and acknowledging that our spiritual liabilities overwhelmingly exceed our spiritual assets. The Lord called it being *"poor in spirit."*

This declaration places both Jesus Himself and His instruction in direct conflict with the modern world which tells us we already have within ourselves everything necessary to develop a blessed life. Twenty-first century writers do not propose that your blessedness comes by acknowledging the complete poverty of your spirit, emptying your heart and mind of self, or declaring the bankruptcy of your soul. To the contrary, their message declares, "Believe in yourself;

recognize your innate powers; express your positive self-confidence, self-reliance, and self-assurance. This will bring you great blessings." Jesus Christ taught the opposite.

The Master declared that the blessed kingdom person begins his walk by admitting, "I have nothing and can do nothing to cover the wrongdoing of my past, provide strength for my present or offer hope for my future. In my spirit (soul) I am bankrupt, destitute, and totally without resources...poverty stricken...a spiritual beggar."

Why this need to declare spiritual bankruptcy? In so doing we openly acknowledge our sinfulness, rebelliousness, and utter lack of any spiritual values capable of making us acceptable to God. An overwhelming sense of inadequacy will flood our heart, and in the words of the poet, August M. Toplady, we can declare, "Nothing in my hand I bring." Now we are prepared to depend totally upon the Lord.

The result? Jesus said, *"...theirs is the kingdom of heaven."* Not 'may be' or 'will be,' but *"is."* What does this *"kingdom of heaven"* represent? Everything that is the opposite of the kingdom of the world. It represents the presence of God...the guidance, power, authority, rule, justice, grace, mercy, righteousness of God. In this kingdom God is in control and the bankrupt *"poor in spirit"* is willing to submit and be governed by God. This destitute soul trusts and obeys God completely because, as Jesus instructed later in His ministry, he has denied himself in order to follow the Master *(Luke 9:23).* Nothing now stands in the way. This poverty-stricken soul can experience the reality of Jesus' presence in his life because God is in control.

In addition, the foundation for future spiritual development has been laid. Now, there is a place for the remaining seven character traits to develop - the 'being' part of the Sermon on the Mount (Beatitudes). With these in place there is no potential for the remainder of Christ's message - the 'doing' part - to be expressed through this person. This follower of Jesus is ready to grow...to become the individual described by the Beatitudes and to live the actions prescribed in the rest of Christ's Sermon.

Upon declaration of your spiritual bankruptcy you, as a fully committed disciple of Jesus, can receive, experience, and enjoy the riches only God gives. Just as Jesus promised, *"theirs is the kingdom of heaven."*

CHAPTER 3

5:4 ... Demonstrate a Repentant Heart

~

"Blessed are those who mourn, for they shall be comforted."

Jesus' introduction of the second Beatitude moves our focus twelve inches lower, from the head to the heart. The kingdom person, according to Jesus, is *"poor in spirit,"* having mentally recognized and acknowledged his complete spiritual bankruptcy. This disciple now transitions naturally to mourning as he wraps his mental acknowledgment with the sorrow of a heart that can no longer control the agony.

This sorrow in the spiritually destitute individual, coming from an anguished mind and broken heart, pours forth in abundance, revealing a truly aching soul. King David's heart expressed such emotion in a variety of ways: *"all the day I go about mourning" (Psalm 38:6); "feeble and crushed" (Psalm 38:8); "heart throbs" (Psalm 38:10); "my pain is ever before me" (Psalm 38:17)*. In similar manner, the apostle Paul's spirit cried out, *"Wretched man that I am!" (Romans 7:24)*.

Even though we see the spiritual bankruptcy of the entire world, it is our own sinful activity and wayward condition that now overwhelms our heart. Understanding our own spiritual poverty produces an emptiness leading to spiritual agony. In this Beatitude Jesus clearly showed us the inevitable result of this hollowness. The recognition of our complete inadequacy before God floods our bankrupt spirit with mourning.

The *"poor in spirit"* kingdom person also sees cause for mourning the lives of others. The prophet Ezra demonstrated such a spirit when, *"he was mourning over the faithlessness of the exiles" (Ezra 10:6)*. Though not personally bankrupt in spirit Himself, Jesus experienced mourning over the waywardness of Jerusalem *(Luke 13:34)*, thus becoming *"a man of sorrows and acquainted with grief" (Isaiah 53:3)*. Likewise, our mourning reaches out to embrace a hollow and hopeless world.

A world focused on fun and pleasure offers a contrary message, as illustrated through the words of an English poet, "Tis impious, in a good man, to be sad"...or the instructions of an old-time song, "Pack up your troubles in your old kit bag and smile, smile, smile." It has even officially declared that we should be involved in "the pursuit of happiness." However, Jesus takes us down a different path, a path of mourning. The Master helps us understand that before we can walk the spiritually glorious path of productive Christian living we must travel through this valley of despair and grief.

To those who acknowledge their bankruptcy and mourn over their condition Jesus promised comfort. He did not say they will be comfortable, but *"they will be comforted."* This comfort comes because, in broken-hearted recognition of our spiritual liabilities, we acknowledge that God and only God can resolve our situation. Therefore, we submit completely to Him. He then brings us comfort through His Word *(Romans 15:4)*, through the encouragement of other disciples *(2 Corinthians 7:6)*, and through the presence and work of the Supreme Comforter - His Holy Spirit - in our lives each day *(John 14:16, 26-27)*.

Thus far Jesus has explained that the only route to real joy comes from acknowledging our spiritual bankruptcy and mourning over it. Why must we experience such sorrow? Because this heartfelt reaction to our mental recognition of spiritual poverty brings us to the feet of Jesus crying, "Lord, I want to be different. I want to be changed. I no longer want to be in conflict with God, ruining my life and the lives of others." With the mourning of a broken heart we have taken the next step beyond a poverty-stricken spirit. We are progressing on the path to productive Christian living...becoming a fully developed kingdom person, a mature disciple of Jesus Christ.

CHAPTER 4

5:5 ... Develop a Humble Spirit

~

Blessed are the meek, for they shall inherit the earth."

Perhaps none of the Beatitudes demonstrates more clearly the dynamic contrast between the world's ideas and the teaching of Jesus than does this third Beatitude.

The Lord stated very plainly, not only will the meek be the blessed ones, they will also inherit the earth. His words are diametrically opposed to the message shouted out by the world: "The strong man gets ahead. The assertive person wins. Demand your rights. Toot your own horn. Wave your own flag. Promote your own goals. Success awaits only those who boldly charge forward and claim it for themselves."

The world not only propounds a message that is the opposite of Jesus' words it ridicules His promotion of meekness. The phrase "meek as a mouse" and characters like Charlie Brown show the disdain of the world for this virtue which the Lord lifts up.

Understanding the true meaning of Jesus' words helps us see the truth He proclaimed. He did not choose a word that portrays a timid, indecisive, wishy-washy, easy-going, easy-to-run-over kind of personality trait. The word used by the Master in this Beatitude, "*meek*," was also used to describe a powerful, soothing medication that quieted a fevered patient or a strong muscular animal submissive to the control of its handler. Jesus' word described power under control, or as one speaker titled it, "Disciplined Strength."

The Teacher Himself perfectly portrayed this spirit of meekness. Jesus did not react in anger when people purposefully mistreated Him. He remained cool and controlled while patiently enduring insults, lies, and injustices. He did not make demands for personal privilege. His inner state of meekness controlled His outer actions. Even when the Master expressed anger it was about the right things, for the right reason, demonstrated in the right way, at the right time, and for the right length of time. Jesus gave us a living picture of this meekness...strength under control.

Kingdom people, truly bankrupt in spirit and overwhelmed with grief because of their spiritual condition, inevitably yield to the spirit of meekness. Knowing we are without spiritual resources in ourselves, we no longer focus on, promote or proclaim self-status. Meekness now controls us.

Acknowledging our complete lack of standing with God and rejecting all inner boasting in our relationship with God, we also eliminate outer boasting in our relationship with people around us. Wrapped in meekness, we recognize the utter ridiculousness of a self-assertive display of power and the foolishness of demanding our rights. Instead, we meekly see the need for and choose to become a humble and gentle person.

As a result of this newfound meekness kingdom people can, as Abraham did in dealing with Lot *(Genesis 13:8-9)*, set aside personal rights for the benefit of others. They can present the message of Christ with *"gentleness and respect" (1 Peter 3:16)*, and seeing a brother caught in sin can *"restore him in a spirit of gentleness" (Galatians 6:1)*. As meek servants of Jesus we become able to *"count others more significant"* than ourselves *(Philippians 2:3-4)*.

Such controlled strength puts a disciple of Christ in complete opposition to the world's belief that the meek will be deprived and run over while the powerful and assertive take control of everything. To the contrary, Jesus declared this willingness to acknowledge one's lack of inherent standing before God and the world, in reality, puts the kingdom person in position to *"inherit the earth."*

A meek disciple of Jesus fully understands this promise from his Master. Upon letting go of everything, laying no personal claim to anything, and admitting a total lack of self–established resources, as a servant of the Lord I now experience the complete satisfaction and contentment found in Christ alone. The words of the apostle Paul, *"All things are yours" (1 Corinthians 3:21)*, become reality through Jesus. No longer do I need to stand up, shout, demand my rights, assert my personality, and grab what I can to get ahead. Rather, having acknowledged a total lack of resources and standing before God as a kingdom person, I now understand that what mankind offers is of no eternal use to me. I delight in the wonderful discovery that in Jesus Christ every need is fulfilled. As a loyal citizen in God's kingdom all that belongs to God is mine to enjoy. By submitting meekly to the Creator I humbly become one with the Master. In this oneness with the Lord I, as a meek servant of God, discover there is no need to be domineering, demanding or assertive for the purpose of obtaining things or gaining control because in Christ I have already inherited the earth.

CHAPTER 5

5:6 … Maintain a Deep Desire for God

"Blessed are those who hunger and thirst for righteousness,
for they shall be satisfied."

The disciple of Jesus, having experienced the first three Beatitudes, moves very naturally into the fourth. Acknowledging spiritual bankruptcy, expressing heart-felt mourning over that condition and its causes, and putting self out of the picture as he meekly falls at the feet of the Master produces in that follower a sense of total emptiness. A deep, inner craving overwhelms this empty soul. Jesus called it a hungering and thirsting.

Hungry and thirsty people know only one desire and they desperately seek a way to satisfy it. Their priority list is short. The pain of hunger must be ended. The parched thirst must be quenched. They want only food and water.

Many in Jesus' audience, being poverty stricken, knew from experience the feelings He described. They understood the reality of surviving from day to day. These people lived in a land which often enveloped them in dryness resulting in scarcity of food and water. They knew what it meant to be hungry and thirsty.

Therefore, Jesus' listeners could understand the picture when He taught, "As a result of your spiritual bankruptcy, your broken-heartedness, and your meekness of spirit you will recognize your great need for the righteousness of God. That need can only be met by seeking His righteousness with the same longing that drives you in seeking food and water when you are starving and parched. To be filled with God's righteousness must become the desperate, all-consuming desire of your body, soul, and spirit. That righteousness must become something you cannot get along without."

The Psalmist portrays this craving when he cries out, *"As a deer pants for flowing streams, so pants my soul for you, O God. My soul thirsts for God, for the living God" (Psalm 42:1,2) .... "And there is nothing on earth that I desire besides you" (Psalm 73:25).* When this sense of spiritual starvation and thirst wells up within our soul and becomes the driving force of our life we will be blessed with the filling that only a disciple of Jesus knows...a filling that completely satisfies the inner craving.

This filling, the *"righteousness"* provided only by God, brings complete blessedness to the soul. The kingdom person enjoys legal righteousness - God's declaration of justification *(Romans 4:23-24)*, moral righteousness - experienced in character and conduct *(Romans 6:13)*, and social righteousness - evidenced in love and compassion shown toward all of the disciple's neighbors *(Mark 12:31)*.

Just as food and water provide necessary nutrition for physical life this *"righteousness"* from God gives strength to the spiritual life. It alone solves the bankruptcy problem, eliminates the mourning, and gives standing to the meek disciple. Only this unique food for the hungering and thirsting soul brings a sense of fullness. It is a satisfaction provided only by *"The Lord [Who] is our righteousness" (Jeremiah 23:6)*. This hungering for the knowledge of God, a relationship with God, and the presence of the righteousness of God will bring a filling from God... *"for he satisfies the longing soul and the hungry he fills with good things" (Psalm 107:9)*. These good things, coming only from God *(James 1:17)*, give that special blessedness reserved for the kingdom person.

Acknowledging spiritual bankruptcy points me toward the kingdom of heaven. Mourning this condition and its causes leads to inner comfort. Meekness takes self out of the picture, causing me to bow in humble obedience to God Almighty, and opens the door of my heart to all God's riches. Hungering and thirsting for righteousness then bring to me the complete fullness only God can provide. The process is complete. Formerly, a citizen of the world, I have become a kingdom person...and the evidence, as Jesus described it in the final four Beatitudes, will be seen by all who observe my productive life as a Christ-like disciple.

surviving from day to day. These peo[illegible]
enveloped them in dryness resulting in [illegible]
They knew what it meant to be hungry and th[illegible]

In Your Relationship With People

CHAPTER 6

5:7 ... Show a Merciful Spirit

"Blessed are the merciful, for they shall receive mercy."

Jesus promised that the disciple who hungers and thirsts after righteousness will be filled. Is there any evidence indicating that filling has occurred? Yes. The next four Beatitudes reveal characteristics evident in the life of the once bankrupt but now filled kingdom person. Imbedded in this follower's character will be a merciful spirit, a pure heart, a commitment to peacemaking, and faithfulness when facing opposition.

We should not be surprised to find a merciful spirit as one of the first visible traits in the disciple of Jesus because it is an ever-present trait in the heart of God. Old Testament scripture overflows with observations about God's mercy, two of which tell us *"his mercies never come to an end" (Lamentations 3:22); "The Lord is good to all, and his mercy is over all that he has made" (Psalm 145:9).* Only because of this mercy in the heart of God can any spiritually bankrupt individual become a filled and satisfied kingdom person. Therefore, it seems reasonable that one who would live as a child of this merciful God would be challenged by Jesus to demonstrate God-like mercy toward others.

Four components hidden within the Lord's simple statement, *"Blessed are the merciful...,"* help us better understand this identifying trait of the kingdom person who is beginning to experience a productive Christian life.

The first component in the need for mercy is a negative condition. Something is not right - there is difficulty, trouble, helplessness, misery. It might even be a disgusting or repulsive condition. This significant negative always indicates the absence of something good, producing the existence of a need to be addressed.

Mercy also requires a positive provision capable of meeting this negative situation. A mercy-giver must have the resources as well as the ability and power to do good for the hurting person. Equally important, a kingdom person who would be merciful must be willing and prepared to bear a cost, make a sacrifice. There cannot be mercy where there is an expected repayment. So, a merciful disciple becomes a willing giver rather than a self-centered taker (Ex: Good Samaritan - *Luke 10:25-37*), often experiencing a personal price physically, materially, emotionally or spiritually.

An unusual component found in the heart of a merciful child of God is the combination of both love and hate...at the same time. There is love for the person needing mercy, but hatred for the circumstance or cause creating the need. The co-mingling of these two produces the merciful spirit. Jude brings the two together when he instructs followers of Jesus first to *"keep yourselves in the love of God"*

(Jude 21), and then *"to show mercy...hating even the garment stained by the flesh" (Jude 23).*

Perhaps the final component is the most demanding - the need for a personal sense of connection between the kingdom person who gives the mercy and the one needing mercy. It requires 'getting into the other person's skin,' seeing what they see, thinking what they think, and feeling what they feel. Compassion, sympathy, empathy...call it what you will, the biggest challenge faced by the kingdom person in being merciful may be the ability and/or willingness to mentally and emotionally become the other person in order to feel their trouble, suffering or misery as they feel it. When that spirit unites with the other components and mercy flows from the heart of Christ's disciple the world witnesses evidence that this truly is a kingdom person.

No child of God will have trouble finding places to demonstrate a merciful spirit. People struggling with basic needs for life can be found wherever we look. Both Old and New Testaments emphasize the need for God's servants to be merciful to hurting souls facing life-disturbing conditions *(Isaiah 58:6-7,9-10; Matthew 25:34-36).*

One scenario rises above all others in challenging the kingdom citizen to be merciful - that difficult moment when someone commits an offense against him personally. Stephen, a servant in the early church, provides an outstanding example of a merciful spirit in this kind of circumstance *(Acts 7:57-60).* He became a living demonstration of words spoken long before, *"Good sense makes one slow to anger, and it is his glory to overlook an offense" (Proverbs 19:11).*

Sometimes mercy is not an easy trait to display. However, for God's kingdom person there is always a motivation that empowers him in granting this gracious gift. It is the mercy this formerly bankrupt soul has already experienced personally. Paul reminded us how

"God our Savior...saved us, not because of works done by us in righteousness, but according to his own mercy" (Titus 3:4,5). Peter echoed, *"According to his great mercy, he has caused us to be born again to a living hope" (1 Peter 1:3).* Realization by this same soul that he will need to receive God's mercy in the future further strengthens the desire to demonstrate a God-like mercy to others.

When I have poured out my bankrupt soul in mourning, in desperation falling meekly before the Lord, I can surely appreciate both the need for and blessing from a gift of mercy. As a kingdom person I should have little difficulty in passing on to another needy soul the kind of mercy God has shown toward me. The Master promised, when I do show that mercy to others, I *"will receive mercy"* ... and it will reveal in a clear way my desire to experience and share the blessing of a productive Christian life.

CHAPTER 7

5:8 ... Concentrate on Purity of Thought

~

"Blessed are the pure in heart, for they shall see God"

In describing *"the pure in heart"* Jesus spoke of individuals who had already experienced a special blessing from God when He *"cleansed their hearts by faith" (Acts 15:9) "from an evil conscience" (Hebrews 10:22).* Because they knew the joy of complete release from the burden of sin and its consequences they could experience the freedom of true purity.

There is more, however, to purity in heart than enjoying a cleansed state of being. Purity of heart also describes the force flowing from that heart which empowers and directs everything in the disciple's life; *"As he thinks within himself, so he is" (Proverbs 23:7) [NKJV]; "Keep your heart with all vigilance, for from it flow the springs of life" (Proverbs 4:23).*

Now there exists a desire to experience this purity to its fullest...to think with a pure mind, to speak with a pure mouth, to function with pure motivation, to live with and know first-hand the blessing that comes to a truly pure heart.

This blessing given to God's pure-hearted servant is special. *Psalm 24:3,4* informs us the one *"who has clean hands and a pure heart"* can *"ascend the hill of the Lord,"* and *"stand in his holy place."* In this Beatitude Jesus described that blessing saying such a person *"shall see God."* How is it that we *"see God"*?

Following an explanation of unclear information we sometimes respond, "Now I see it," meaning we know it and understand it. To see God is to know and understand Him. It is to develop spiritual vision, producing the ability to comprehend in a new and more complete way the God we love and serve. The pure heart can personally connect with the pure and holy God. In this Beatitude Jesus announces that this special gift of seeing God is only promised to those who are pure in heart...the result being that pure-hearted kingdom people can have an understanding of God that people of the world do not experience *(1 Corinthians 2:14-17)*.

This kingdom person, purified by the cleansing blood of Jesus Christ and living by faith, will see God everywhere he looks. The pure in heart sees God in nature *(Psalm 19:1)*, in history *(Psalm 105; Acts 4:24-28)*, in life's circumstances *(Genesis 45:5-8)*, in fellow humans *(Genesis 1:27; Acts 17:26-29)*, and most of all in Jesus Christ *(John 14:9)*. This pure-hearted servant has a new perspective on everything in life, a cleansed view free of the sinful world and its debilitating influence. Now, he understands the truth of Paul's words: *"To the pure, all things are pure" (Titus 1:15)*. Because the light has dawned the pure heart sees things as God sees them.

Seeing...knowing...understanding God, the *"pure in heart"* becomes an imitator of God *(Ephesians 5:1)*. Seeing the true nature of God and comprehending His loving and giving spirit, this formerly self-centered person becomes a selfless giver. Through both this process and the resulting actions the pure-hearted disciple is being *"conformed to the likeness of his Son" (Romans 8:29)*...experiencing continued purification even *"as he (Jesus) is pure" (1 John 3:3).*

No greater blessing can come to me in this life than to experience a truly pure heart. When motivated by such Christ-like purity I will develop a vision of God through which I sense His presence wherever I go in His world. Furthermore, I and all other pure-hearted kingdom people can look forward to a complete and perfect vision of God when we are taken where *"nothing unclean will ever enter" (Revelation 21:27).* We will be at the *"throne of God and of the Lamb"* where we *"will worship him"*...and truly *"see his face" (Revelation 22:3-4)* in a way that supersedes anything we experience with Him in this world.

CHAPTER 8

5:9 ... Become a Peacemaker

"Blessed are the peacemakers, for they shall be called sons of God."

The Bible opens portraying a peaceful garden of Eden and closes with the picture of a peaceful new Jerusalem. Between these two descriptions we find over four hundred references to peace. So, it should not surprise us to hear the Master promising a special blessing to His peacemaking disciples. It is a natural activity for the kingdom person.

The God worshipped by kingdom people is a God of peace *(Romans 15:33; 1 Thessalonians 5:23)*. Our Master preached peace *(Ephesians 2:17)* and brought peace through the cross *(Colossians 1:20)*. It is this peace in Jesus *(John 16:33)* that the Holy Spirit produces in the disciple's life *(Romans 14:17; Galatians 5:22)*.

The peace of God enjoyed in the lives of His servants does not exist in a vacuum. The pure heart previously mentioned by the Lord provides a nest for a peace-loving spirit *(James 3:17)*. Experiencing the filling that comes as a result of hungering for righteousness allows the follower of Jesus to understand why the Psalmist united the two, saying, *"righteousness and peace kiss each other" (Psalm 85:10).*

Unfortunately, we live in a world where peace is often talked about but seldom truly experienced. One historian reported that between 36 BC and 1968 AD there were 14,553 recorded wars. In spite of its claimed desire for peace our society erects monuments to warriors. Movies, books and TV programs do not become big sellers by focusing on peacemaking. Even games soar to the top of the popularity list by offering opportunities to participate in electronic violence, fighting, and wars. Man spends time talking about peace while he reloads his weapons. Obviously, a desperate need for the peacemakers Jesus described exists in our sin-laden homes, neighborhoods, work places, entertainment areas, governments, and, unfortunately, sometimes even churches.

To become a blessed peacemaker one must first be wrapped in the blanket of peace. The primary material used in creating this very special blanket is the kingdom person's knowledge that they personally are at *"peace with God through our Lord Jesus Christ" (Romans 5:1)*. Only a person at peace with God can become an effective peacemaker.

Once God's servants are wrapped in the peacemaker's blanket they enjoy a unique blessing sought by multitudes. The peace of God *"guard[s] [their] hearts and [their] minds in Christ Jesus" (Philippians 4:7)* and *"rule[s] in [their] hearts" (Colossians 3:15)*. Therefore, they experience the great blessing of being at peace with themselves. The combination of peace with God and with self equips kingdom people to begin peacemaking in the world around them, their *"feet, having put on the readiness given by the gospel of peace" (Ephesians 6:15).*

Now fully equipped, peacemakers can demonstrate their commitment to peace *"so far as it depends on [them]"* by living *"peaceably with all" (Romans 12:18)*. These kingdom servants set the example for others to follow as they seek peace when confronted with conflict in their own personal relationships *(Matthew 5:23-24; 18:15-17)*. By being *"at peace with one another"* the disciples of Jesus prepare themselves to be powerful salt in the world *(Mark 9:50)*. Now they can effectively help others *"be reconciled to God" (2 Corinthians 5:20)* by telling *"the good news of peace through Jesus Christ" (Acts 10:36)*. These Christ-ians become truly blessed peacemakers as they guide people to peace with God through Christ and help them make peace with one another.

The Master teaches that I and all other peacemaking kingdom people can properly *"be called sons of God."* Why? As peacemakers we have become *"imitators of God...as beloved children" (Ephesians 5:1)*. Our lives demonstrate full participation in *"the divine nature" (2 Peter 1:4)* of a peace-loving and peace-making God. As *"sons of God"* who *"strive for peace with everyone, and for the holiness" (Hebrews 12:14)* we learn that *"those who plan peace have joy" (Proverbs 12:20)*. The combined impact of all the preceding Beatitude character traits grows me into a fully developed disciple of Jesus, a productive peacemaker, who personally discovers *"there is a future for the man of peace" (Psalm 37:37)*.

CHAPTER 9

5:10-12 ... Practice Patient Endurance

"Blessed are those who are persecuted for righteousness' sake, for theirs is the kingdom of heaven.

"Blessed are you when others revile you and persecute you and utter all kinds of evil against you falsely on my account. Rejoice and be glad, for your reward is great in heaven, for so they persecuted the prophets who were before you."

Surely, disciples of Jesus who personally experience and demonstrate each of the first seven Beatitudes will be loved and accepted by all. Right? Wrong! Jesus declares the opposite is true...not acceptance, but rejection; not approval, but disapproval; not praise, but persecution. The true kingdom person learns very quickly, develop the first seven Beatitudes and you are guaranteed to experience the eighth - open, direct, and personal opposition.

Jesus alerted His followers to the certainty of this response by saying, *"WHEN others revile you and persecute you,"* not 'if' *(5:11)*. Godliness generates hostility, antagonism and animosity. Scripture is filled with examples of this fact: Abel worshipping *(Genesis 4)*; Jeremiah prophesying *(Jeremiah 37 & 38)*; Daniel praying *(Daniel 6)*; the Apostles preaching *(Acts 4)*; Stephen witnessing *(Acts 7)*. The apostle Paul fully understood the words of Jesus, speaking from experience when he wrote, *"Indeed, all who desire to live a godly life in Jesus Christ will be persecuted" (2 Timothy 3:12)*.

The Master gives two reasons for this active rejection of His disciples. Ironically, that for which a kingdom person hungers *(5:6)* becomes part of the foundation for the world's hostility - *"persecuted for righteousness" (5:10)*. Everything about God's way of righteousness is opposite to the unrighteousness of the world. Even these Beatitudes illustrate this fact. Declaring spiritual bankruptcy goes contrary to the world's self-development mantra. Why mourn?…"You have the right to be happy." Meekness?…"That's weakness." Hunger for righteousness?…"Do your own thing; set your own standards." Show mercy?…"You will be walked over." Be a peacemaker?…"Stand firm on and for your own rights." The two ways are as different as light and darkness *(John 3:19-21)*.

The second reason for opposition given by the Lord focuses on Himself - *"…utter all kinds of evil against you falsely on my account" (5:11)*. He referred again to this scenario later in His ministry: *"If they persecuted me, they will also persecute you….all these things they will do to you on account of my name." (John 15:20,21)*. It is all about Jesus, *"the way, and the truth, and the life" (John 14:6)*; *"the blessed and only Sovereign, the King of kings and Lord of lords" (1 Timothy 6:15)*; *"the Alpha and the Omega, the first and the last, the beginning and the end" (Revelation 22:13)*. Be religious, talk about God or be active in a church...that is acceptable. But become one with the Lord Jesus Christ, lift up the name of Jesus and openly acknowledge Him as your Master and, as a kingdom person, you will guarantee your own rejection by the world. You will be laughed at, ridiculed, insulted, slandered and persecuted.

How should God's servants react to this rejection? The apostles set the example for all kingdom people when *"they left the presence of the council, rejoicing that they were counted worthy to suffer dishonor for the name" (Acts 5:41).* They followed the instruction of Jesus Who taught His followers how to respond to opposition: *"Rejoice and be glad," (5:12).* An accurate translation of these words could be, "I command you to rejoice and continue being exceedingly glad."

Negative responses to opposition do not fit in the life-style described by Jesus. He gives his followers no room for self-pity, grumbling, complaining of bad treatment, or any other negative reaction to opposition and persecution. Scripture continually instructs them to always respond with joy and satisfaction for the opportunity to *"share his sufferings" (Philippians 3:10).*

Jesus also provided the reason for rejoicing and being glad: *"... for theirs is the kingdom of heaven...for your reward is great in heaven," (5:10,12).* Only two other New Testament verses use both of these words together - *"rejoice...be glad [exult]"* - and both refer to the day *"when his glory is revealed" (1 Peter 4:13)*, and when *"the marriage of the Lamb has come" (Revelation 19:7).* These writers join with Jesus in redirecting our attention from the present rejection to the future reward; the time when today's persecution will turn to praise, and hateful hostility will be replaced with approval and acceptance.

Rejoicing in opposition and persecution becomes a realistic reaction for me when I understand my *"slight momentary affliction is preparing for us an eternal weight of glory beyond all comparison, as we look not to the things that are seen but to the things that are unseen. For the things that are seen are transient, but the things that are unseen are eternal." (2 Corinthians 4:17-18).* This leads me to the blessedness Jesus promised to every persecuted kingdom person and empowers me to walk the path of productive Christian living.

CHAPTER 10

5:1-12 ... Beatitudes Summary

As Jesus promised in each Beatitude, when these character traits come alive in the personal experience of the Lord's servants they will enjoy the blessednesses only God can give. However, the greater blessing in these truths is best seen when they are considered as a unit.

These Beatitudes reveal the fundamental spiritual traits of a kingdom person. The characteristics Jesus described here are to be manifested in all of His disciples. These traits, whether looked at individually or as a unit, provide a clear delineation between a kingdom person and a person of the world. They describe the life of God's servant who has a grasp of the eternal and the meaningful in a world of shallow and superficial options.

Secondly, we note that there is no randomness in these statements. The Beatitudes move in an orderly progression, explaining the development of a person's spiritual life.

The first four Beatitudes introduce us to the fundamental process in becoming a kingdom person. First, there is the acknowledgment of spiritual bankruptcy *("poor in spirit")* followed by a heartfelt godly repentance *("mourning").* These lead to an attitude toward God *("meekness")* which produces a craving *("hunger... thirst")* for that which addresses the bankruptcy problem - the perfection of God's righteousness.

With our roots firmly planted in the righteousness of God, we are shown that the Lord's servant begins producing fruit identifying him as a follower of the Lord Jesus Christ. Knowing his only standing with God is through grace the kingdom person is compelled not only to rely on God's mercy, but to display God's mercy in his own relationship with others. The purity of the disciple's heart makes this possible and empowers him to become a peacemaker among people, both in the body of Christ and in the world.

The result of this experience, however, is not what the disciple might expect. The sin-darkened world which rebelled against and attacked the Teacher of the Beatitudes also rejects His followers whose daily lifestyle grows out of these Beatitudes. God's servants discover that this path begins in spiritual poverty and ends in persecution. Therefore, it becomes a path which the world, unlike the kingdom person, will not accept as a highway to blessedness.

These characteristics described by Jesus, however, are more than a description of the way to blessedness. They also give a complete picture of servanthood...what produces it, how it is displayed, and what it produces.

The foundation for servanthood - to be *"poor in spirit"* - produces the reaction of servanthood - *"mourning"* - and leads to the strength of servanthood - *"meekness."* The desire of servanthood - *"hunger and thirst after righteousness"* - prepares the Christian to be *"merciful"* - the demonstration of servanthood. The protection of servanthood - being *"pure in heart"* - equips the believer for the opportunity of servanthood - being a *"peacemaker"* - leading to the unexpected result of servanthood - being *"persecuted."* The enticement toward the servanthood resulting from each of these characteristics described by the Master is the opportunity to experience the unique blessedness which only God gives and only the true kingdom person enjoys.

In these Beatitudes Jesus revealed the kind of person His servant is to be. The remainder of the Sermon on the Mount shows how these principles apply in the real situations of daily life - what His servant is to do. For example, Jesus teaches one who hungers and thirsts for righteousness *(5:6)* to make this the priority of his concerns even if the basic necessities of life are at stake *(6:28-34).* Again, a peacemaking disciple *(5:9)* learns how this spirit specifically impacts worship when conflict enters his life *(5:23-24).*

A final observation of the Beatitudes shows that they all grow directly out of obedience to the two greatest commands - loving God and loving neighbors *(Mark 12:30-31).* When those two commands come alive in the kingdom person's spirit that individual will become a walking picture of the Beatitudes, and will experience a productive Christian life.

[Note: In preparation for our examination of the remainder of the Sermon on the Mount you will find it helpful to identify each of the Beatitudes in the column of your Bible with B-1, B-2, B-3 ... to B-8.]

CHAPTER 11

5:13 - 7:27 ... Living the Beatitudes

A careful reading of the Sermon on the Mount immediately reveals that the kingdom lifestyle as described by Jesus is in continual conflict with the world's lifestyle. The kingdom person, being a living picture of the Beatitudes, soon realizes the impossibility of walking with one foot in God's kingdom world and the other foot in mankind's natural world. There is no similarity. They are opposites.

Using simple statements of fact, illustrations, and plainly stated instructions and commands the Master Teacher revealed the clash between the two life-styles. He touched every corner of life, demonstrating the contrast between kingdom living and worldly living. In the process Jesus clearly showed how the kingdom person addresses life's situations. His life-applications can be categorized as follows. [Note that each topic is connected to specific Beatitudes.]

Matthew 5:13-16 ... The kingdom person's influence (B-8)

" 5:17-20 ... Genuine greatness (B-4)

" 5:21-26 ... Relationships (B-7)

" 5:27-30 ... Inner Purity (B-6)

" 5:31-32 ... Marital Loyalty (B-3, B-5, B-7)

" 5:33-37 ... Integrity (B-6)

" 5:38-42 ... Reactions (B-3, B-7, B-8)

" 5:43-48 ... Imitating God's Love (B-6, B-7, B-8)

Matthew 6:1-4 ... Benevolent Generosity (B-1, B-6)

" 6:5-13 ... Prayer (B-1, B-2, B-6)

" 6:14-15 ... Forgiveness (B-5)

" 6:16-18 ... Heartfelt Devotion (B-1, B-2, B-6)

" 6:19-24 ... Life Focus (B-4)

" 6:25-34 ... Contentment/Priorities (B-4, B-8)

Matthew 7:1-5 ... Self-examination (B-5)

" 7:6 ... Protecting the Sacred (B-8)

" 7:7-8 ... Assurance (B-4)

" 7:9-12 ... Reciprocal Living (B-5)

" 7:13-14 ... Destiny (B-4)

" 7:15-20 ... Spiritual Alertness (B-4)

" 7:21-23 ... Obedience (B-4)

" 7:24-27 ... Lifetime Wisdom (B-4)

" 7:28-29 ... The Authority (B-4)

The life experiences and teachings of Jesus recorded in the remainder of the Gospels provide additional illustrations and amplification of these life topics. In fact, proceeding step by step through the entire New Testament Scriptures reveals a pattern in the way God's truth about kingdom life is presented. The Beatitudes, as a description of what a disciple of the Master is to be, provide a foundational connection to the rest of Jesus' teaching in the Sermon on the Mount, an explanation of what that follower is to do. The truths in this Sermon then find further amplification in Jesus' own life experiences and additional teaching as revealed by the four writers of the Gospels. Finally, application to real-life situations comes to us through specific examples and expanded instruction given by the remaining New Testament writers.

For example, the Lord's explanation about contentment and priorities in life *(6:25-34)* amplifies Beatitude #4 *(5:4)*. Additionally, the way He dealt with the rich young ruler *(Luke 18:18-30)* illustrates how this teaching impacts real life situations. Furthermore, the apostle Paul's words to Timothy *(1 Timothy 6:6-10, 17-19)* provide specific commentary on the ultimate result of applying Jesus' instructions to life's daily practicalities.

Hopefully, following this pattern will lead us to a more complete understanding of the Christian's kingdom lifestyle as we continue our examination of the path to productive Christian living.

THE LIFESTYLE OF THE PRODUCTIVE CHRISTIAN

5:13-20

The Impact of the Christian Life

CHAPTER 12

5:13 ... Like Salt

~

"You are the salt of the earth, but if the salt has lost its taste, how shall its saltiness be restored? It is no longer good for anything except to be thrown and trampled under people's feet."

The Beatitudes pictured for us the spiritual character of Jesus' disciple. Surprisingly, the Master's next words give neither directive instructions nor commands. Rather, He makes a simple statement of fact - *"You ARE..." (5:13,14).* The Christlike believer's influence is automatic. The Lord explains how this kingdom person, a walking picture of the Beatitudes, impacts the surrounding world. The Teacher describes that impact in very specific ways - it is like *"salt"* and *"light."*

Salt has been a common and important commodity in society for thousands of years. That salt does a variety of things is well known around the world. Spread salt on ice and it causes the ice to melt away, but rub it into meat and it becomes a preservative. Put salt in food and a desirable flavor is created, but pour it into a wound and its cleansing power results in severe pain. Interestingly, the commodity itself remains the same in each situation. The kind of impact/influence salt has is determined by the environment into which it is placed.

So it is with the disciple of Jesus. The believer's character remains the same in all circumstances, but the nature of that kingdom person's impact will vary, depending upon the environment into which it is placed. For example, the salt of Jesus' righteousness melted the cold heart of an uncaring and oppressive tax collector *(Luke 19:1-9)*. Paul, however, hoped that the Master's righteousness expressed through his own life and writing would work as a salty preservative in the battle against the rot and decay developing in the Corinthian church *(2 Corinthians 7:8-10)*. When Barnabas allowed the Lord's righteousness to work as salt through his life it brought the wonderful flavor of loving acceptance into the body of Jerusalem believers *(Acts 9:26-30)*. However, the apostle John explained to believers that when their Christ-like righteousness came into contact with an unbelieving and unrighteous world it would be like salt in an open wound causing that world to retaliate against them *(1 John 3:11-13)*.

Regardless of the environment one principle is at work in all circumstances. The presence of salt impacts every situation. It is inevitable. Jesus did not say, "You can be"...or..."You may be"...or..."You should be...". He said, *"You ARE the salt of the earth."* Wherever His disciple goes, whatever the situation, that kingdom person who is a walking picture of the Beatitudes will, like salt, always influence the surrounding environment. The nature of that influence will vary, depending upon the situation, but it is always present.

However, even salt can lose the power to influence its surroundings, or as Jesus described it, *"has lost its taste."* Why does that happen? Something is wrong with the salt. Outside impurities mix with the salt, destroying its ability to act in a beneficial way on its environment. When that occurs, salt becomes utterly useless and is tossed aside.

Such a picture presents a strong warning to the kingdom person. Do not let outside impurities enter your life and destroy your role as a presenter of righteous influence in an unrighteous world. Should that happen, you become useless to the kingdom, unable to positively impact the world for God. So, keep yourself open to God's power in order that the Beatitude traits will live and grow in your life.

The Master stated it plainly, "You, and you alone are the salt of the earth." As a disciple of Jesus I have the power to be God's genuine salt in this decaying world. So long as I and my fellow believers function as salt we can impact the world. However, if we allow impurities to enter our lives we will stop working as God's salt at home, in the school, around the neighborhood, on the job or in society. We will lose our usefulness in the Lord's work. I must be aware, as Jesus cautions very clearly, He will not be pleased if my 'salt-power' as a kingdom person evaporates into nothingness.

CHAPTER 13

5:14-16 ... Like Light

~

"You are the light of the world. A city set on a hill cannot be hidden. Nor do people light a lamp and put it under a basket but on a stand, and it gives light to all in the house. In the same way, let your light shine before others, so that they may see your good works and give glory to your Father who is in heaven."

Scripture tells us that *"God is light" (1 John 1:5)*. In his Gospel John declares that Jesus was the *"true light...coming into the world" (John 1:9)*, and he later records Jesus' own declaration, *"I am the light of the world" (John 8:12)*. The apostle Paul speaks of *"the kingdom of his beloved Son,"* also calling it *"the inheritance of the saints in light" (Colossians 1:12-13)*.

God is light. Jesus became God's visible light in the world, resulting in the kingdom introduced by Jesus becoming a kingdom of light. Therefore, we should not be surprised to hear Jesus tell kingdom people, *"You are the light of the world" (5:14)*.

Jesus had already addressed the influence of His followers in the world when He said they are *"the salt of the earth" (5:12).* Just as He used the functions of salt to describe the impact of His disciples on the world Jesus now uses light to further emphasize His servants' role.

The primary purpose of light is to dispel darkness. In so doing, light enables people to see what surrounds them and to gain knowledge of their situation. Light also helps people see what is ahead, where to go and what to avoid. Light helps a person comprehend their environment so they can make meaningful and purposeful decisions. In short, light provides the illumination which enlightens one's understanding of their circumstances, making it possible to act appropriately.

This is the role of a kingdom person in the world. Believers wrapped in 'Beatitude garments' automatically illuminate the sin-darkened world around them. Jesus does not tell them to be light, to become light, or to act like light. Jesus states very plainly, *"You ARE the light...." (v.14).* That is the inevitable result of a kingdom person putting on the Beatitudes.

The sole instruction Jesus gives to His followers is, *"let your light shine before others" (v.16).* Don't hide it; don't hinder it; don't cover it. Put it out there so people can see it. But where is 'there'? Where is *"before others"*?

If the role of light is to illuminate or dispel darkness then it must be placed where the darkness is in order to fulfill its purpose. The *"before others"* where light should shine is out in the world of darkness. Light only accomplishes its intended purpose when it is thrust into the darkness.

Unfortunately, many kingdom people allow their light to shine only around other kingdom people. Servants of the Lord who truly want their light to fulfill its intended purpose must step into the kingdom of darkness - a sinful world - where that light becomes meaningful. Light added to light only makes the light a little brighter. When light is injected into darkness the darkness is eliminated and people living in darkness are given opportunity to see, understand, and respond appropriately to their environment.

How do kingdom people function as light in the kingdom of darkness? Many would say, "By proclaiming the message of light." Certainly, this is a necessary activity, but Jesus did not focus on that process. He described the means of shining one's light in a very specific way - *"that they may see your good works" (v.16).*

Where do those good works come from? Any servant wrapped in the Beatitudes will automatically produce good works. A person declaring spiritual bankruptcy before God...relying totally on God... experiencing repentant sorrow over the presence of sin...radiating meekness and humility...hungering for God and His righteousness... demonstrating mercy...maintaining a pure heart...actively engaging in peacemaking...and willingly standing firm in the face of opposition and persecution, will not be hidden in society. Their good deeds will stand out like a lighthouse in a sin-darkened world, dispelling darkness, illuminating and giving meaning to life and serving as a guide for others. Their uniqueness will be recognized by all.

Such a servant becomes the vehicle through which the light of God shines. Thinking people...people who ask, 'Why?'...people who seek causes...will consider the good works displayed by the Beatitude-wrapped kingdom person and realize these can only be attributed to the power of God. This is the ultimate purpose of letting your light shine...of being the light of the world. Point people to God. Bring people to the feet of the Master.

What, specifically, are the good works which people see in this Beatitude-wrapped kingdom person that result in their praising the God of light and His Son, *"the light of the world"*? The Master describes those very clearly in the remainder of the Sermon on the Mount.

Summarizing Jesus' use of light to illustrate the role of kingdom people, we would suggest there are only two reasons for darkness. There is no light - it simply does not exist - or there is light, but it is hidden. In either case people are left groping in darkness. Hiding a light completely contradicts its purpose, providing illumination for people in darkness. Therefore, Jesus declares, hiding our light as His followers is not an acceptable choice. Jesus did not say, "You can be....", "You should be...", or "You might be....". The Master said to kingdom people, *"You ARE the light of the world."* Clearly, Jesus expects us to impact the sin-darkened world through the influence of our productive Christian life.

The Controlling Influences in the Christian Life

CHAPTER 14

5:17-19 ... Foundation: God's Enduring Word

~

"Do not think that I have come to abolish the Law or the Prophets; I have not come to abolish them but to fulfill them. For truly I say to you, until heaven and earth pass away, not an iota, not a dot, will pass from the Law until all is accomplished. Therefore whoever relaxes one of the least of these commandments and teaches others to do the same will be called least in the kingdom of heaven, but whoever does them and teaches them will be called great in the kingdom of heaven."

As Jesus moved into the 'directive instruction' phase of the Sermon on the Mount He began by announcing the foundational truth upon which He would build all that followed. It was the absolute which would undergird His followers of all eras...the reality of authority.

The Lord described the unwavering authority upon which His own life was built, and explained that the citizens of His kingdom must build upon that same authority. In confirming the nature of God's law Jesus directed His followers to God's word as the unalterable guide for their lives. Soon He would examine six areas of life as guided by God's law, but the Master Teacher first established the enduring nature of God's word.

The disciples of Jesus heard Him proclaim that what God has declared will endure until everything in God's plan is fulfilled *(5:16)*. The Lord assured kingdom people at the beginning of their venture that the foundation they stand upon - God's enduring word - will not fail or end until everything God intends to accomplish is completed. God's enduring word spans all of time, making it relevant in all ages up to the end.

Jesus further strengthened the validity of God's enduring word by declaring His life would be a complete fulfillment of that word *(5:17)*. In no way did He intend to eliminate or alter God's message to man. Rather, people of His day would observe its complete fulfillment as they saw the Lord confront both ordinary and extraordinary circumstances of life. If God's people wondered what was intended in the law given by God they could see its meaning being lived out in the life of their Master. Jesus' daily life became the visible demonstration of God's will applied to every situation people face *(John 6:38)*. It was and is the pattern for people of all nations and all time.

The Master further explained that those followers who practice and teach what God has given in His word will travel the road to greatness in His kingdom *(5:19)*. In giving this clear statement, Jesus informed kingdom people that, like His, their lives are also to be a living demonstration of God's will applied to daily situations. His servants are called to walk in His footsteps in surrendering to the will of God as expressed through His word.

Why are Christians called to follow this path? One who adheres to the law of God, daily living out the word of God, builds up the kingdom of God through his lifestyle. This demonstration of loyalty to God and His instruction lifts one to the level of greatness in God's kingdom *(5:19).* A kingdom person who loyally heeds the instruction coming from God demonstrates his own wisdom *(7:24)*, proves his love for God *(John 14:15,21,23)*, and experiences the assurance of knowing he has a living relationship with God *(1 John 2:3-6)*. This is productive Christian living at its best.

This foundational truth given by the Master - the enduring nature of God's law - is simple, but profound. It tells me that I can effectively function as a follower of Jesus when I duplicate His example in my own full commitment to the enduring word of God. My profound respect for and submission to the law of God, growing out of my acknowledgement of spiritual bankruptcy, meekness, and hunger for righteousness, will lead me to live that word, becoming the salt and light of the world.

However, a warning is needed. It is possible for me to express this commitment to the righteousness of God and His enduring word in an unacceptable way. Therefore, Jesus explains in His next statement the need for me to act with great caution.

CHAPTER 15

5:20 … Objective: Genuine Righteousness

"For I tell you, unless your righteousness exceeds that of the scribes and Pharisees, you will never enter the kingdom of heaven."

Jesus earlier promised that those who *"hunger and thirst for righteousness"* will be filled, experiencing God's special blessedness *(5:6)*. In His statement currently under consideration the Master explained that the righteousness expected of His followers differs greatly from the righteousness people heard described and saw in the lives of their own teachers. In addition, He made clear that only a righteousness superior to what they had heard about and saw would provide entrance into the kingdom of heaven.

According to Jesus the lives of *"the scribes and Pharisees"* clearly illustrated an inadequate righteousness. His hearers must have considered this to be an astounding declaration because these men were considered by many to represent the pinnacle of personal piety. One Jewish observer declared, "If only two people go to heaven one will be a Pharisee and the other a teacher of the law." Many hearers must have been shocked to hear Jesus say, "If your righteousness does not exceed that of these men you don't stand a chance of getting into God's kingdom." What could possibly be wrong with the righteousness of the Pharisees and teachers of the law?

Perhaps the most obvious shortcoming of their wholly inadequate righteousness was its extreme focus on the external. They carefully and deliberately practiced valid religious activities in specific ways, but for the purpose of drawing public attention to their 'piety' *(6:2,5,16)*.

A second weakness showed itself in the continued emphasis on ceremonial practices developed over the years by their own religious leaders *(Matthew 15:1-3)*. These had become so sacred they were put on the same level as the things of God, and taught as if they were the commands of God. In their opinion, men who ignored such traditions could not possibly be walking on the right path in life.

Self had become the center of their righteousness *(Matthew 23:5-7)*. They concentrated on the things THEY liked, activities THEY wanted to do, and experiences THEY enjoyed rather than what God wanted. Theirs had become a religious system designed to develop good feelings about themselves, as is illustrated by the Pharisee who *"...standing by himself prayed thus: God I thank you that I am not like other men..." (Luke 18:11)*.

They allowed a righteousness attained by works to replace the desire for personal spiritual development of the heart and a living relationship with God. The Pharisees and teachers of the Law focused on activities rather than attitudes, programs rather than principles, and doing things right (according to their definition of 'right') rather than being the right kind of person. Sadly, their attitudes and practices still live in today's religious world.

The end product from this type of righteousness was a group of people who were extremely religious, seen by many as very pious, and highly regarded for their external spiritual lifestyle. Unfortunately, that righteousness fell far short of the kind of righteousness expected by Jesus.

What was missing in the righteousness of the Pharisees and teachers of the law? God's words through two of their own ancient prophets, Jeremiah and Ezekiel, give a strong clue. *"I will put my law within them, and I will write it on their hearts" (Jeremiah 31:33). "I will put my Spirit within you" (Ezekiel 36:27).* Jesus' words in the Beatitudes add clarification to the issue, *"Blessed are the pure in heart" (5:8).* Christ further strengthened this when He identified the most important command, *"You shall love the Lord your God with all your heart...." (Matthew 22:37).* The Lord's apostles continued that emphasis, teaching believers to do *"...the will of God from the heart" (Ephesians 6:6).*

The contrast between the two kinds of righteousness becomes clear. The righteousness of the Pharisees focused on the external. The righteousness Jesus described in the Sermon on the Mount was rooted in the heart. His was not just a righteousness of actions. His was a righteousness which completely changed the person from the inside out, resulting in a dramatically different approach to everything in life.

The Master Teacher emphasized this significant distinction in the instruction which followed immediately...an instruction given in the form of antitheses - *"You have heard....But I say to you."* Each one of the six antitheses focuses on a heart issue: *5:21-26*... Relationship and Reconciliation; *5:27-30*...Inward Purity; *5:31-32*... Marital Loyalty; *5:33-37*...Personal Integrity; *5:38-42*...Priorities: People over Possessions; *5:43-48*...Motivation: Be Like God.

Each of Jesus' antitheses showed how the righteousness He proclaimed exceeded the righteousness taught by the religious leaders of His day. Theirs was a righteousness developed by piling human goodness upon human goodness, then refining it, polishing it, and perfecting it. His, on the other hand, started in the spirit of the man and grew outward, producing a life patterned after the Master Himself.

The life of righteousness described by Jesus in each antitheses would stand out in both the religious and secular worlds. His righteousness would be a living demonstration of the Beatitudes. Its impact would be like salt and light in the world. Its foundation would be the enduring word of God. The crowds were about to learn how the righteous and productive life of the Master's servant would be dramatically different from the righteousness proclaimed by the Pharisees.

The Attitudes of the Productive Christian 5:21-48

The Relationship Attitude

CHAPTER 16

5:21-22 ... The Nature of Relationship Problems

"You have heard that it was said to those of old, 'You shall not murder, and whoever murders will be liable to judgment.' But I say to you that everyone who is angry with his brother will be liable to judgment; whoever insults his brother will be liable to the council; and whoever says, 'You fool!' will be liable to the hell of fire."

Jesus began His instruction in the Sermon on the Mount describing the character of a kingdom person (Beatitudes). Then the Lord described the impact of the kingdom person (preserve as salt, illuminate as light), the foundation upon which the kingdom person stands (God's enduring word), and the fruit produced in a kingdom person's life (righteousness that exceeds the righteousness of the Pharisees). From this point on we could describe His teaching with these words: "...and here is how to do it in real life."

Using antitheses *("You have heard...But I say")* the Master Teacher turns His hearers' attention toward six practical areas of life. The first antithesis must have surprised them: *"You have heard... You shall not murder" (5:21).* A listener in that crowd might have thought, "Why does He bring up that issue? We are not a crowd of murderers. Certainly, I am not guilty of murder. I am a righteous person." With that reaction the hearer would have moved to the exact spot where Jesus wanted him to stand. Such a mindset prepared the hearer for the primary lesson.

Unexpectedly, Jesus changed the emphasis. He moved from the outward action *(5:21)* to the inner attitudes *(5:22).* He addressed specific attitudes known and experienced by every person in the crowd at some time in their life: a brooding, simmering, grudge-holding, resentful, bitter anger that refused reconciliation; a contempt, disrespect and derision that could think of or treat a person as an 'idiot, numbskull, blockhead, nitwit, or bonehead'; a judgmental spirit which evaluated another as a spiritual rebel with inadequate standing before God.

Suddenly, the previously innocent, self-righteous listener was forced to acknowledge an unpleasant fact. His perceived righteousness disappeared quickly. His innocence turned to guilt. The righteousness of his outward action was buried by the unrighteousness of his inner attitudes.

The Master Teacher refocused the issue by declaring, "Even though you have not physically killed someone, in your heart and mind you have had the same thoughts as the murderer holds. Mentally, internally, deep within your heart you have done the same thing the murderer does...you have attacked a person created in the image of God, and, therefore, you are subject to the same judgment."

A thinking hearer would have understood immediately what Jesus meant earlier when He said, *"Unless your righteousness exceeds that of the scribes and Pharisees…" (5:20)*. It was crystal clear. The righteousness which the Master sought was an internal righteousness. In man's world, "They can't put you in jail for your thoughts." Not so in God's world. In the world of God's kingdom His servant's heart must be right…it is expected to be *"pure" (5:8)*.

Jesus introduced these people to a deeper, more meaningful way of understanding God's instruction. When God forbids an act of sin He, at the same time, is forbidding all the attitudes which produce that act, even if the attitude never develops into an action. To use a simple illustration: If it is wrong to harvest corn, then it is wrong to plant the seed; it is wrong to water the seedling; it is wrong to cultivate the plant.

We now begin to understand what Jesus meant by living a righteousness which exceeds that normally accepted by man. The Lord of the kingdom tells us, "If you are going to be My disciple you are expected to live on a much higher plane than this world considers acceptable. You must look beyond your actions into the very core of your being. It is there that you experience the righteousness of which I speak."

Had the Master taken a poll after His first statement, *"You shall not murder,"* not a single person would have declared, *"I am guilty."* All would have felt righteous. If He had followed His second statement with a poll all would have been forced to raise their hands, acknowledging their guilt. The words were written later by Paul, but on that day all would have had to acknowledge with him, *"None is righteous, no, not one" (Romans 3:10)*.

With the first antithesis Jesus clearly illustrated for His disciples the dramatic difference between living in His kingdom and the kingdom of this world. He helped them understand that man's normal way of viewing life is not acceptable to the kingdom person. The focus must go deeper than the outward action; it must go to the inner core of one's being.

In understanding the need for this righteousness that exceeds even that of the world's most righteous people, I, as a kingdom person, must quickly acknowledge I am faced by an insurmountable obstacle. No person, including myself, operating with mere human resources can live the righteous life being described by the Master. This kind of kingdom living requires divine power. Therefore, if I seek to live by the Master's standard I must throw myself at the Master's feet, and humbly *(5:3-5)* seek the righteousness which only God can provide *(5:6)*.

CHAPTER 17

5:23-24 ... The Importance of Addressing Relationship Problems

~

"So if you are offering your gift at the altar and there remember that your brother has something against you, leave your gift there before the altar and go. First be reconciled to your brother, and then come and offer your gift."

Jesus' first antithesis focused on the kingdom person's relationships. Beginning with the most obvious and worst outward reaction in a human relationship - murder *(5:21)* - Jesus refocused His hearers attention upon their inner reactions to other people - attitudes of the heart *(5:22)*. One might expect the Lord's instruction about relationships to end at this point. However, again He refocused their attention.

The Master Teacher moved skillfully toward the ultimate relationship of kingdom people - their relationship with God - showing that relationships with fellow human beings have a direct connection to their relationship with the heavenly Father. Jesus' specific instruction suggested His followers cannot have a good relationship with God if they have a broken relationship with one another. So significant is this issue that the Lord instructed, "If you have a broken relationship with another person put God on hold until you make an attempt to resolve that problem. After you have addressed the issue with that person you can come back before God, offer your worship and strengthen your relationship with Him."

In the process of presenting the conclusion to His first antithesis Jesus helped us understand two truths often overlooked by His disciples. First, relationships between Jesus' followers are so important they should take precedence over acts of worship. Secondly, worship involves more than simply bowing down before God and presenting an offering to Him. True worship includes proper preparation.

Our immediate reaction to the first truth might be one of doubt or disbelief. How can anything be more important than worshipping God? How can it ever be right to turn away from an act of worship in order to do something else? Jesus' instruction provides clear answers to these questions.

Two specific people are the characters in this 'drama.' The first is *"you [who] are offering your gift at the altar,"* a kingdom person... one who has determined to surrender his life to the authority of Almighty God and express this submission through worship.

"Your brother," may include every other human being, but certainly identifies a fellow kingdom person, specifically the one who *"has something against you" (5:23).* Who might that be? A brother whom you have offended. How? Jesus does not even address that issue. It does not make any difference. Who cares what you did or did not do? When the relationship has broken down because of your action, real or perceived, Jesus instructs us to make an attempt at

reconciliation. This is the natural objective for a kingdom person clothed in the Beatitude that promises: *"Blessed are the peacemakers, for they shall be called sons of God" (5:9).*

This peacemaking effort, however, involves more than interpersonal relationships. In the second principle presented the Master connects the attempt at reconciliation with the kingdom person's worship of the Father. *"Offering your gift at the altar"* is an act of worship. In view of that fact Jesus surprises us with His instruction. "Stop! Don't continue your worship effort... '*Leave your gift...go.*'"

Who would ever expect the Master to say, "Make God wait"? But He does. He plainly and clearly declares, *"First be reconciled..." (5:24).* Reconciliation must precede worship. According to Jesus this matter is so vital the kingdom person must interrupt their public act of worship, attempting first to reconcile and enjoy peace with their fellow kingdom citizen.

It is difficult for us to conceive of anything more important than worshipping God. Jesus, however, does tell us when the heart is polluted with animosity, bitterness, and anger against someone, or the knowledge that someone believes we have offended them, clearing up that offense with a brother in the kingdom is more important than appearing at God's throne for worship.

The instruction is quite plain. I must interrupt my worship. Put God on hold. Keep God waiting. Go away and address the problem. God will wait for me to return. It is my responsibility to demonstrate genuine Christlike spirituality and love. I must face the person and resolve the problem, bind up the broken heart, comfort the dejected soul, seek forgiveness and offer forgiveness. Then I can come back with a cleansed heart and a mended relationship to worship God.

The Father will be waiting, ready to receive my worship...a worship that truly fulfills the two great commands *(Mark 12:29-31).* Knowing that my personal relationships and my relationship with God stand on solid ground, I can discover the blessing of a congruent life lived in harmony and unity with others. I can experience the joy of worshipfully bowing with a pure and peaceful heart in humble adoration and praise before a holy God, at the same time further developing my productive Christian life.

CHAPTER 18

5:25-26 ... The Urgency of Addressing Relationship Problems

"Come to terms quickly with your accuser while you are going with him to court, lest your accuser hand you over to the judge, and the judge to the guard, and you be put in prison. Truly I say to you, you will never get out until you have paid the last penny."

Given the choice between fixing a broken piece of furniture or approaching someone for the purpose of fixing a broken relationship most people would opt for the furniture. Why? It is easier to analyze and understand a problem with things than with people. The solution is more obvious. The result of a repair effort with the furniture is more predictable, and that effort will probably not make the situation worse.

Attempts to repair broken human relationships can present difficult and challenging dynamics. Identifying and understanding the problem is not always easy. The solution may evade us. Results from the efforts to repair broken relationships are far from predictable, and sometimes carry the potential of making matters worse. Therefore, we often avoid repairing broken interpersonal relationships...or at the very least, we postpone the effort.

Jesus knew that even kingdom people would face this struggle. So, in closing His instruction regarding the first antithesis - addressing personal relationship issues - our Lord emphasized the need to *"come to terms quickly" (5:25).*

Some wonder why the Master introduced a legal situation - being taken to court - as an illustration for His instruction. Perhaps it is because that clearly shows a broken interpersonal relationship carried to the extreme. Highly moral, civilized people would not consider murder *(5:21).* However, a relationship might reach such a point of dysfunction that these same people might go against a brother in court.

Jesus' illustration imagines such a situation...progressing from difficult to bad to worst case scenario. How did it get there? Through the refusal of someone to properly address the broken human relationship.

After explaining one of the problems with broken relationships...they hinder your ability to worship God *(5:23-24)*...the Master addressed a second problem. Broken relationships unaddressed rarely resolve themselves. Rather, they tend to grow continuously worse and can result in extremely serious consequences.

The Hebrews writer reaches into the world of nature to illustrate the same point. *"See to it...that 'no root of bitterness' springs up and causes trouble, and by it many become defiled" (Hebrews 12:15).* People sometimes try to keep broken interpersonal relationships, like roots, hidden beneath the surface. Unfortunately, also like roots, they seldom stay there. The problems grow, producing plants (additional trouble) and fruit (impacting others). Sometimes that impact is extensive, defiling many. We have all seen it happen...a small misunderstanding serves as the seedling from which a root of unrest develops. Then, growing into a tree of conflict it branches out into many other issues, involving people not a part of the original problem. For that reason the writer of Hebrews encourages kingdom people to put on their Beatitude clothing *(5:7)* when he instructs them to *"Strive for peace with everyone" (Hebrews 12:14).* Furthermore, like Jesus, he shows that this does impact one's relationship with God: *"...without (holiness) no one will see the Lord" (Hebrews 12:14).* Elsewhere, positive direction from the apostle Paul provides specific steps to help the kingdom person deal with these issues and become both a peacemaker and an imitator of God *(Ephesians 4:29-5:2).*

A summary of Jesus' instruction in the first antithesis helps Christians understand the need to address broken relationships in a serious way. First, Jesus explains the nature of this problem, sinful attitudes in the heart, putting the offender in the same category as murderers and in danger of facing eternal consequences *(5:21-22).* Secondly, He shows that the kingdom person's relationship with God is negatively effected, even making acceptable worship impossible until the issues are addressed *(5:23-24).* Finally, the Master reminds His followers that delay in dealing with the interpersonal problem will inevitably lead to further destruction of the relationship and extremely serious consequences *(5:25-26).*

In essence, Jesus explains to me, "Mr. Christian, understand that My disciples address relationship issues differently from people of the world. If you are involved in a broken relationship, especially with another kingdom person, remember this problem impacts even your relationship with God, and left unaddressed will only get worse. So, be proactive. You need to take steps immediately and address the issues even before you worship. Restore harmony. As a kingdom person demonstrate that you truly are the peacemaker of the Beatitudes. Settle matters quickly. Do it now!"

The Inner Purity Attitude

CHAPTER 19

5:27-28 ... Purity Begins in the Heart

"You have heard that it was said, 'You shall not commit adultery.' But I say to you that everyone who looks at a woman with lustful intent has already committed adultery with her in his heart."

How are the following verses related to the words Jesus spoke at this point in the Sermon on the Mount? (a) *Matthew 13:17* - *"... many prophets and righteous people longed to see what you see..."* (b) *Philippians 1:23* - *"...My desire is to depart and be with Christ..."* (c) *1 Thessalonians 2:17* - *"...with great desire to see you..."*

Each verse contains the word Jesus used in *5:28* in His description of a man who *"looks at a woman with lustful intent." "Longed to see"* (a), *"desire"* (b), and *"great desire"* (c) are translations of the same basic word Jesus used when He described looking at a woman *"with lustful intent."*

These Biblical texts show us two important facts about this word. First, it is a neutral word. It expresses an attitude that in itself is neither good nor bad, neither right nor wrong, neither righteous nor sinful. It simply describes an attitude expressed by intensely focusing on a specific object or purpose. It pictures one who dwells on an object/purpose, deliberating with the deep desire of experiencing whatever the object, goal, or end result can bring into that person's life.

Therefore, we learn secondly, that it is the object being focused upon that determines the acceptability or unacceptability of the desire. If you desire or have an intense longing for the right object, it is a good attitude. Longing for or lusting after the wrong object is a sinful attitude.

In this second antithesis *("You have heard...But I say to you")* Jesus again went beyond the outer action and addressed the attitude of the mind and heart. He clearly indicated there is a problem with desires that are focused on the wrong object...in this case, another man's wife.

The similarity between the first and second antitheses is clear. Each begins by addressing an outward action...murder or adultery. As when He mentioned murder, most people in Jesus' crowd would immediately respond in their mind, "I am OK; I have not committed adultery." But again the Master Teacher dug into their inner beings and addressed the issue at its source...the place where even those innocent of doing the wrong action would, nevertheless, find themselves confronted by the problem of harboring wrong thoughts.

While the Lord spoke specifically in this antithesis of the act of adultery, in reality He reached back to the sixth Beatitude - *"Blessed are the pure in heart..." (5:8)* - and addressed what happens when that Beatitude is not present in His follower's life. Indeed, purity of heart would protect a kingdom person from holding or cultivating a lustful desire in his heart for another man's wife.

A thinking kingdom person, however, also would realize that the instruction Jesus gave regarding looking lustfully on a woman has a much wider application. He would know that one can be led astray by the *"the desires of the eyes" (1 John 2:16)* in a variety of ways. For example, the outward disobedience of Eve in the garden began when she *"saw that the tree was…a delight to the eyes…" (Genesis 3:6).* God chose to close the Ten Commandments not only with a warning about coveting a neighbor's wife, but also his *"house…or anything that is your neighbor's" (Ex 20:17). Micah 2:2* tells us that people coveted (lusted for) fields and their fellowman's inheritance.

No event illustrates these words of Jesus better than David's unholy involvement with Bathsheba. The word 'lust' does not appear in that Biblical record, but clearly it was present in David's heart, and it began through the 'lust of his eyes' when he saw a beautiful woman bathing *(2 Samuel 11:2)*. Do we really need it described in print to understand that David did exactly what Jesus described… *"already committed adultery with her in his heart" (5:28)*?

So how does a kingdom person maintain the inner purity described by the sixth Beatitude...a purity that stands in the way, blocking attitudes and activities addressed by Jesus in this antithesis?

Job set a good example when he committed himself to control the focus of his eyes: *"I have made a covenant with my eyes; how then could I gaze at a virgin?" (Job 31:1).* Had David done the same he would have avoided a lot of trouble.

Paul encouraged us to avoid an environment that cultivates lustful thinking when he wrote, *"For it is shameful even to speak of the things that they do in secret" (Ephesians 5:12).* Combining these words with Job's terminology we might declare: "Make a covenant with your tongue not to talk about what Paul calls *"unfruitful deeds of darkness" (Ephesians 5:11)*."

Fences and guards may keep Christians away from places where they ought not to be, but pure hearts and positive thoughts will have a stronger effect in assuring that they hold to Jesus' teaching. As a believer I will find it easier to maintain purity of heart when I set my mind *"on things that are above" (Colossians 3:2)* and *"on the things of the Spirit" (Romans 8:5)*. When I truly dress in the fourth Beatitude by hungering and thirsting *"after righteousness" (5:6)* I will find it easier to keep my mind focused on things that are *"true ... honorable ... just ... pure .... lovely ... commendable" (Philippians 4:8)*.

As Christ's followers we can be assured that where a pure heart presides there will be no longing for or lusting after the wrong things. Desires leading to sinful acts can be eliminated at their source. Maintaining my purity of heart will conquer desires that can destroy a productive Christian life.

CHAPTER 20

5:29-30 … Maintain Purity Regardless of the Cost

~

"If your right eye causes you to sin, tear it out and throw it away. For it is better that you lose one of your members than that your whole body be thrown into hell. And if your right hand causes you to sin, cut it off and throw it away. For it is better that you lose one of your members than that your whole body go into hell."

A well-known national preacher received great attention from both religious and secular media when he claimed there is no hell. That attention was not because the writer's ideas were new or unique. Indeed, they have been proposed for centuries. As one reporter described it, he was getting this attention because unlike most of the 'no-hell' proponents of the past this writer was not part of the liberal wing of Christianity. He was what people describe as, "a Bible-believing evangelical." Really?

The Bible records Jesus clearly speaking about hell in this text and elsewhere in Scripture *(Matthew 10:28; 18:9; Mark 9:44).* So, how can a writer who openly denies there is a hell be called a "Bible-believing evangelical"?

Our Lord teaches one thing; someone proposes the opposite. This puts a very simple question before us. Whom do we believe, Jesus or this someone? The answer is equally simple. Jesus is the Son of God, the Christ, the Lord...our Lord. What any other person proclaims does not make any difference. True kingdom people believe what Jesus said even if it creates issues or dilemmas they do not understand. Hell is not the only topic Jesus spoke about that presents us with unanswered questions. Having unanswered questions does not mean we have to doubt what He taught. It does mean that we acknowledge our own fallibility as human beings and then continue to anchor our faith in a Lord who does understand it all.

What we do understand very clearly is that Jesus said hell was such a terrible place people should do whatever is necessary to stay out of it. The illustrations the Master Teacher used to make that point are quite stunning. "Avoid hell at all costs," He declared, "even if to accomplish that you must gouge out your eye or cut off your hand." Jesus certainly knew how to be dramatic.

Was the Lord really instructing people to literally take out an eye or cut off a hand? Whether you answer that 'yes' or 'no' the meaning of what Jesus taught remains the same. Any sacrifice in life is worth the cost if the sacrificed object stands in the way of enjoying eternal fellowship with God. Whatever does or does not occur here, Jesus declares no price is too high to pay in order to avoid being separated from God in this place called hell.

Jesus helps kingdom people understand that in all places at all times eternity is more important than the present, purity is more important than pleasure, right priorities are more important than possessions. We learn from Him that any worldly attitude, desire, action, object, program or process that leads us into eternal spiritual ruin needs to be taken out of our life immediately with surgical precision. The Master tells us we must become uncompromisingly adamant in removal of everything destructive to our soul.

The Lord of all explains, "Your eyes may be valuable, but not as valuable as your eternal soul. Your hands may be valuable, but not as valuable as your eternal soul. If you have to give up anything to save your soul from the destination of eternal separation from God, no matter how important it is to you, then give it up! Be it a hobby, a habit, a friend, a job, a business, a possession, an attitude, a lifestyle, even a family relationship *(Matthew 10:37)*...cut off anything that leads you into sin and the ultimate destruction of your soul in separation from God."

The idea that there is a hell which is an horrendously terrible place and that we should take extreme steps to avoid did not come into existence at some conference table of religious leaders. It was Jesus, the Son of God, the same Person who told us about heaven, Who also told us about hell.

One of the interesting realities of the Christian community is that most people who call themselves Christians believe what Jesus teaches about a place called heaven. However, according to several surveys a significant percentage of the same people don't believe what Jesus teaches about a place called hell. Ironic, isn't it? Choosing to believe Jesus Christ in the first case, then choosing not to believe Him in the second. It appears that the spirit of old Israel still lives: *"Speak to us smooth things, prophesy illusions...let us hear no more about the Holy One of Israel" (Isaiah 30:10,11).* Disciples should always remember that the Person Who taught us about hell is the same Person Who taught us about heaven. If we cannot believe Him about one how can we believe Him about the other?

The Lord used an extreme illustration, a dramatic attention-getter, to tell us, "It is better to lose anything in this world, even what is personally precious to you, and be My faithful servant than to have anything or everything you want and be eternally separated from God." The alternative to eternal fellowship with God is terrible beyond description. "People," Jesus declares, "avoid hell at all costs!"

The Marital Loyalty Attitude

CHAPTER 21

5:31-32 ... Maintaining Marital Loyalty

~

"It was also said, 'Whoever divorces his wife, let him give her a certificate of divorce.' But I say to you that everyone who divorces his wife, except on the ground of sexual immorality, makes her commit adultery. And whoever marries a divorced woman commits adultery."

Some topics are always relevant. Marriage and its related issues is one of these, confronting people of all societies in every century. In these verses Jesus addresses divorce, an issue faced by many conflicted couples. The Lord gave additional instruction on this topic at other times in His ministry *(Matthew 19:7-9; Luke 16:18)* as did the apostle Paul *(1 Corinthians 7:27)*. Anyone who has studied these and other related Scripture texts knows any writer can use many pages to consider all the ramifications associated with Biblical teaching regarding the marriage-divorce issue. That will not be done here.

However, the title of this chapter introduces one part of the issue which we can address both directly and simply.

Inherent in the marriage relationship is the certainty of disagreement and conflict. Sometimes these grow to such proportions that the people involved in the problem face three options: 1 - Continue living in an unhappy marriage; 2 - Divorce [At another time in His ministry Jesus clearly stated this circumstance occurs "... *because of your hardness of heart" (Matthew 19:8).* Heart-hardening results in at least one of the partners, sometimes both, closing the door completely on the possibility of choosing the third option.]; 3 - Maturely face up to the personality problems, mishandled issues and personal hang-ups that created difficulties in the marriage and deliberately choose to take positive steps toward building a strong marital relationship.

Even though no marriage can completely avoid the entanglements of disagreement and conflict a couple can avoid options #1 and #2 by carefully cultivating attitudes and actions which lead to a strong marital structure. Loyalty can be maintained and divorce can be avoided when the marriage structure is built on three foundation stones.

First foundation stone: Build the marriage on the right kind of love. Emotional and physical love are both legitimate expressions of the human personality, but neither will result in a strong marriage relationship. The love described in Scripture is a love of choice in which the lover seeks always to do what is best for the person loved, expressing itself through an action described by the Lord's instruction later in this message *(7:12).* Such is the kind of love Jesus Christ chose to show toward His church, and which Paul indicated a husband should have for his wife *(Ephesians 5:25-29).*

Paul shows that Jesus proved His love for the church by willingly sacrificing Himself for it. Why would He do that? Because He and the church are one; it is His body *(Ephesians 5:23).* What was the Lord's objective? To remove all the stains, wrinkles and blemishes and make it a perfect church *(Ephesians 5:26-27).*

Likewise, the right kind of love for his wife in a husband's heart will be demonstrated in his willingness to sacrifice himself for her... to think of her needs ahead of his own in the manner described elsewhere by Paul *(Philippians 2:2-4).* Why? Because he and his wife are one *(Ephesians 5:31).* What is his objective? To remove the imperfections in their relationship so they can enjoy a healthy, mature, loving home.

Paul describes the practical application of this self-sacrificing spirit in the 'Love Chapter' of the Bible (*1 Corinthians 13:4-8*...read it with marriage in mind). Both partners applying this kind of love in their relationship will see significant changes occur in their marriage in a very short time.

Second foundation stone: Recognize the unending necessity of forgiveness. While most people are quick to admit they are not perfect and need to be forgiven, many tend to forget that their imperfect partner also needs forgiveness. Nothing is more totally destructive of a marriage relationship than the refusal to forgive. Forgiveness is hard, especially when Paul's instruction about love is ignored: *"Love...keeps no record of wrongs" (1 Corinthians 13:5) [NKJV].* That seems unfair because it eliminates the opportunity to even things out. Forgiveness is challenging because the carnal satisfaction which comes from sweet revenge is not fulfilled and, potentially, leaves the forgiver feeling short-changed.

Like the love described in Scripture, forgiveness does not come naturally. It also is a choice...in fact, three choices. It is the result of choosing not to bring the offense up to the offender again. Why? Because in the act of forgiveness the debt has been erased, eliminating any reason for further confrontation. Forgiveness is also the result of choosing not to bring the offense up to third parties because the purging of that debt leaves nothing to discuss with them. Finally, it is the result of the forgiver choosing not to dwell on the offense in their own mind. Because they have wiped out the debt there is nothing to dwell upon and, therefore, they choose to focus their thoughts on positive things *(Philippians 4:8).*

Third foundation stone: Both the husband and wife choose to work toward a common goal. That goal must be bigger than themselves or any materialistic accomplishment. One wife describing her own marriage difficulties said, "After we married we had nothing to hold our marriage together except ourselves, which is never enough." In like manner, many couples have discovered all the things of the world are not enough to produce the satisfaction that makes a marriage last.

What goal will hold a marriage together? Jesus gave it as the number one purpose in life, which also makes it the number one objective for a marriage. *"You shall love the Lord your God with all your heart...soul...mind...strength" (Mark 12:30).* Elsewhere He called this *"the great and first commandment" (Matthew 22:37).* When this becomes the primary goal in a marriage the couple has a standard by which they can measure everything occurring in their relationship.

Do you want an absolute guarantee that your marriage will never end in a divorce? Love each other with the right kind of love. Acknowledge and fulfill the never-ending need to forgive. Make loving *(Mark 12:30)*, obeying *(John 14:15,21)*, and honoring God in everything you do *(1 Corinthians 10:31)* the modus operandi for your marriage. Build on this foundation and you will maintain your marital loyalty and avoid a divorce, a blessed accomplishment in the productive Christian life.

The Integrity Attitude

CHAPTER 22

5:33-37 ... Maintaining Integrity

"Again you have heard that it was said to those of old, 'You shall not swear falsely, but shall perform to the Lord what you have sworn.' But I say to you, Do not take an oath at all: either by heaven, for it is the throne of God, or by the earth, for it is his footstool, or by Jerusalem, for it is the city of the great King. And do not take an oath by your head, for you cannot make one hair white or black. Let what you say be simply 'Yes' or 'No'; anything more than this comes from evil."

In the first three antitheses *("You have heard...But I say")* of the Sermon on the Mount Jesus addressed relationships *(5:21-26)*, inward purity *(5:27-30)*, and marital loyalty *(5:31-32)*. He then spoke to kingdom people about integrity, still another issue faced in every society.

Jesus began by addressing the accepted practice of His day *(5:33)*. If a person used God's name when taking an oath it was believed God became a partner in that oath *(Exodus 22:10-11; Deuteronomy 6:13)* and, therefore, it was absolutely binding and a serious sin to violate that pledge. People also believed not using the name of God excluded Him from the oath, thus creating a loophole which provided a defense when the oath-taker violated his pledge.

Taking advantage of this belief people began swearing by anything of major significance in life, such as heaven, earth, Jerusalem, or even their own head. Since the name of God was not included they felt no sense of obligation or loyalty to their oath or to the truth. This led to a system of deceit and duplicity in which oaths would be used not only to hide dishonest intentions, but even to support falsehoods. Excluding God's name, oath-takers believed they successfully protected themselves by acting according to the letter of the law, even though they were ignoring the spirit of the law.

The Master Teacher completely rejected this as a realistic possibility, giving two very clear reasons - the inclusion issue and the exclusion issue - to support His teaching.

Inclusion issue: God is connected to everything *(5:34-35)*. Heaven is His throne, all of earth is His footstool, and the holy city, so-regarded by Jewish people, belongs to Him. So, God is automatically included even when only these earthly things are named as the foundation for an oath.

Exclusion issue: An oath-taker has no power to exclude what is reality in the world. Jesus' example declares, "Artificially make the hair any color you choose, but underneath that tint the natural color of the hair remains. Likewise, an oath-taker cannot remove things in life by simply declaring them eliminated or by ignoring them." Neither can God be excluded from a situation through the simple action of omitting His name from an oath. God's world is what it is and, unlike God *(Genesis 1:3)*, no man can change things by the use or non-use of words.

Many philosophers of the world also address the importance of truthfulness. However, their reasons for encouraging integrity differ significantly from the Master's reasons.

The world bases its motivation for living by the truth-telling principle upon social and personal foundations. It tells us that when deceit and a lack of integrity prevail society will be chaotic, unable to protect anyone from fraud. Ample evidence exists to support this argument in cases where businesses have lied about their products, media has lied about their facts or sources, government employees have lied about their actions, and even church leaders have lied about their behavior. Because this lack of integrity does irreparable harm to society we are told it is important to always be truthful.

The world also explains that being truthful will create a less complicated life for us personally. There will be no need to cover up or explain what we say. One lie, we are warned, will lead to another which will make it hard to remember what we said. We are also cautioned that people won't trust any of our words once they learn we lie.

Social and personal reasons certainly provide good motivation for maintaining our integrity. However, a kingdom person lives up to the 'truth-standard' for more important reasons. A disciple of Jesus Christ follows One of Whom it was said *"there was no deceit in his mouth" (Isaiah 53:9)*. The Lord clearly described His own relationship to truth when He stated, *"I am the truth" (John 14:6)*. Therefore, a kingdom person can only *"be conformed to the image of [God's] Son" (Romans 8:29)* by being totally committed to truth.

The kingdom person, a faithful follower of Jesus Christ, holds to this truth-telling standard because as a child of the one true God he seeks to imitate his Father *(Ephesians 5:2).* We are told in His Scripture that our God, *"delight[s] in truth in the inward being" (Psalm 51:6),* and that *"lying lips are an abomination to the Lord" (Proverbs 12:22).* He also states very clearly that *"all liars"* will be destined to experience *"the second death" (Revelation 21:8)* where they can associate with *"the father of lies" (John 8:44).*

The inconsistency of claiming to be a follower of Jesus Christ and a child of God while at the same time being dishonest and deceitful plainly conflicts with principles Jesus already stated in the Beatitudes. Can one who *"hunger(s) and thirst(s) for righteousness" (5:6)* be anything other than completely truthful? To be *"pure in heart" (5:8)* necessitates the removal of all deceit. Is it possible for kingdom people to practice deceit, creating strife, causing division, and producing distrust, anger and hate between people, and at the same time be called *"peacemakers" (5:9)*?

Clearly, if I am to be a true follower of Jesus I must be committed to the truth; walking in the truth, adhering to the truth, and telling the truth. As one of the Master's disciples I will make every effort to eliminate even the smallest seed of deceit from my heart, words and actions. Like my Lord I must always seek to be a person of integrity. My 'yes' must be 'yes', and my 'no' must be 'no' if I want to experience a productive Christian life.

The Reaction Attitude

CHAPTER 23

5:38-42 ... Controlling Reactions

"You have heard that it was said, 'An eye for an eye, and a tooth for a tooth.' But I say to you, Do not resist the one who is evil. But if anyone slaps you on the right cheek, turn to him the other also. And if anyone would sue you and take your tunic, let him have your cloak as well. And if anyone forces you to go one mile, go with him two miles. Give to the one who begs from you, and do not refuse the one who would borrow from you."

We live in a day of tremendous emphasis upon rights...civil rights, women's rights, prisoners' rights, children's rights, employees' rights, and now even animal rights. Such a strong focus on this issue leads to several problems, including one every person faces when dealing with others. Whose rights are more important? Yours, or mine?

Interestingly, in presenting the fifth antithesis *("You have heard...But I say to you")* Jesus went straight to the heart of the 'rights' issue. Through the use of four illustrations the Master explained that for kingdom people life's situations should not elicit concern about rights. Rather, He focused the attention of His servants on their reactions. Why?

The only way a kingdom person can truly demonstrate that he is a servant of the Lord is by his reactions to life situations. With words a disciple can proclaim his loyalty, but only through his daily response to circumstances can the follower of Jesus prove he is truly a servant of the King. A crucial place for demonstrating this evidence is in the way a disciple reacts when his rights are challenged. Rather than giving a simple statement of principles the Master Teacher chose four illustrations to help His servants understand appropriate reactions by kingdom people.

When speaking of being struck *"on the right cheek" (5:39)* Jesus was probably referring to the back-hand slap delivered with the attackers right hand. This action, when done publicly, was considered demeaning, contemptuous and a gross indignity. So, it appears that Jesus was telling His disciples, "You may feel the need to respond defensively when someone attacks your dignity. At such times don't react like people of the world who feel compelled to protect their image. There is no need to respond in that manner because, as a kingdom person, you stand on a different foundation. Your personal dignity comes from who you are, a child of the heavenly Father, and no one can destroy that or take it from you. Retaliation on your part is not necessary. Such a response proves only that you still think and act like a person of the world."

The cloak mentioned by Jesus *(5:40)* was addressed specifically in Jewish law which clearly stated this garment, if taken from a man, must be returned to him by sunset *(Exodus 22:26-27).* Thus, the owner could easily declare that keeping possession of his cloak was a legal right. But the Master instructed kingdom people to react differently. Here He taught them to voluntarily relinquish that which they had a legal right to claim as their own. Why this reaction? In the first place, a follower of Jesus already relinquishes ownership of all possessions when he becomes a kingdom citizen. Those possessions, as with everything related to the person of the disciple of Jesus, belong to the King. Secondly, even Old Testament law assured that the concern of a compassionate God could be counted on to take care of the one who had no cloak *(Exodus 22:26-27).* Therefore, the appropriate reaction of the kingdom person is to willingly let go of what has not been theirs since they surrendered all to follow the Master, thus demonstrating their faith in God to provide for all their needs.

Jesus' third illustration addresses one's reaction to demands made on time and service *(5:41).* Governments of Jesus' day commonly exercised authority over people's time and even their personal service. The word *"forces"* used by Jesus in this text is the same word Luke used to describe the demands made by Roman soldiers upon Simon from Cyrene when they required him to carry the cross of Jesus *(Luke 23:26).* When facing similar and often unreasonable demands upon their time and service kingdom people are instructed by the Lord to react without resistance and give more than is required.

Not all situations involve protecting dignity, legal rights or responding to authoritative commands. Some develop as the result of simple requests made in ordinary activities of life. Jesus' final illustration addressed the kingdom person's reaction in this kind of circumstance *(5:42).* The fundamental principle found in the first three illustrations continues through the fourth. Regardless of the situation, forced or voluntary, kingdom people should react as servants, foregoing their own rights and acting voluntarily and generously to meet the needs of others.

The heart of the Master's instruction in this fifth antithesis can be summarized in three steps. First, let go of 'your rights.' You no longer have any. You died to self and everything about you now belongs to the Father...you, your body, your possessions, your time, and your service. Stop trying to protect what you no longer hold. Second, reject revenge and renounce retaliation. They are sinful actions typical of the world. Third, think about your witness. You are now a servant of the King and a citizen of the kingdom. You are *"meek" (5:5)*, *"merciful" (5:7)*, *"pure in heart" (5:8)*, and a *"peacemaker" (5:9)*. You are the *"salt of the earth"* and the *"light of the world" (5:12-13)*. Let everyone see how differently a Christ-like 'Beatitude person' responds in a sinful world. Show them through your reactions that you are part of *"a chosen race, a royal priesthood, a holy nation, a people for his own possession"* who through their lives *"proclaim the excellencies of him who called you out of darkness" (1 Peter 2:9)*. Let them see the *"new spirit of your minds"* and *"the new self, created after the likeness of God in true righteousness and holiness" (Ephesians 4:23,24)*. Give them the opportunity to *"see your good works and give glory to your Father who is in heaven" (5:16)*.

Paul later expanded the Lord's instruction, including an explanation of the reason why Jesus' followers need not retaliate or seek revenge *(Romans 12:17-21)*. Neither the Master nor Paul suggested this is an easy road to travel. To the contrary the writer of Hebrews describes kingdom people who suffered greatly because they exemplified this teaching of Jesus in real life situations *(Hebrews 10:32-34)*. Even though a life-situation may not always be pleasant at the surface those who truly react like genuine kingdom people are assured they will experience special blessings *(5:11-12; Hebrews 10:35-36)*.

The title of a booklet published many years ago summarizes the heart of the 'rights vs reactions' issue addressed by Jesus in this antithesis. It is a simple but powerful statement: "Pardon, Your Reactions Are Showing." Upon reading the comments of that writing I found myself confronted by a simple but powerful question: "What do your reactions show?" Perhaps the instruction by Jesus, the Master Teacher, is confronting you with the same question.

The Love Attitude

CHAPTER 24

5:43-48 ... Practicing Perfect Love

"You have heard that it was said, 'You shall love your neighbor and hate your enemy.' But I say to you, Love your enemies and pray for those who persecute you, so that you may be sons of your Father who is in heaven. For he makes his sun rise on the evil and on the good, and sends rain on the just and the unjust. For if you love those who love you, what reward do you have? Do not even the tax collectors do the same? And if you greet only your brothers, what more are you doing than others? Do not even Gentiles do the same? You therefore must be perfect, as your heavenly Father is perfect."

Be perfect!

Now there's a challenge that will get your attention. "No way!" you respond. "Me, perfect? Without flaws? You have to be kidding. Impossible! I never have been and never will be perfect."

But that is exactly the challenge Jesus gave to kingdom people...and He did not stop with the call to perfection. He added, *"as your heavenly Father is perfect" (5:48).* If it is possible, Jesus made the impossible even more impossible. But did He?

The perfection of which the Master spoke was not the flawless condition we normally picture when the word 'perfect' is thrown at us. Our Lord described completeness and full maturity in the expression of god-like love toward those around us. He gives His followers a picture of spiritual growth and development that duplicates the Father's love for all people, excluding no one. The disciple becomes *"perfect"* - mature, complete - in love when he, like his heavenly Father, wraps his love around everyone, including enemies.

In this sixth antithesis *("You have heard...But I say to you")* Jesus addressed the fundamental issue that undergirds each one of the previous antitheses...love. This complete and mature love which duplicates the love of the heavenly Father provides the foundation upon which all of the Lord's instruction stands. Every interpersonal issue faced by kingdom people can be addressed in a Christ-like manner when the heart is controlled by the God-like love described in this antithesis. Like everything else the Master taught in the Sermon on the Mount this teaching stands in stark contrast to what the world believes and practices.

The mature and complete love described by Jesus presents an amazing instruction regarding who is to be loved... *"your enemies" (5:44).* Most people believe it is right to love family, neighbors, friends, the poor, and a host of others. However, for those same people love has limits. They would tell us some individuals do not deserve being given expressions of love, especially one's enemies. The Master, however, declares, "There are no limits to the kingdom person's love. You should love your enemies; yes, even the people who persecute you." Our Lord exemplified His own teaching by loving His enemies, the people who were giving Him trouble. So, if a kingdom person wants to practice that complete, mature love which Jesus taught and exemplified they must begin by loving the people who oppose them and give them trouble.

How do kingdom people show this love? By acting as *"sons of [their] Father in heaven" (5:45)*,...by loving as God loves. The God Who is love *(1 John 4:16)* demonstrates His love through actions, pouring out His blessings not only upon people who please Him, but people who displease Him *(5:45)*. The supreme example of God's perfect love was demonstrated when He acted by sending Jesus to save sinners *(Romans 5:8)*. Likewise, a kingdom person demonstrates the complete maturity the Master desires by showing his love through actions - *"do good...bless...pray for...give...lend...be merciful"* - all of this toward *"those who hate you...curse you...abuse...strike... take away [from you]" (Luke 6:27-36)*. Jesus summarized this action expected of a mature *("perfect")* kingdom person quite succinctly, *"as you wish that others would do to you, do so to them" (Luke 6:31)*.

These responses described by the Lord are totally unlike the world's. Therefore, when mature kingdom people express their love in these unusual ways they get the world's attention, accomplishing two things. First, they identify themselves as true Christ-ians: *"By this all people will know that you are my disciples, if you have love for one another" (John 13:35)*. Secondly, they fulfill Jesus' earlier instruction: *"Let your light shine before others, so that they may see your good works and give glory to your Father who is in heaven" (Matthew 5:16)*.

The level of spiritual maturity described by the Lord in this final antithesis requires serious commitment. It is not within my power as a normal human being to fulfill this expectation. It requires self-denial, is self-sacrificing, puts others above self, and establishes the goal of being like Christ and imitating the Father...all of which I, as a kingdom person, am instructed to be and do *(Luke 9:23; Philippians 2:3-4; Romans 8:29; Ephesians 5:1).*

It does not take long for us to discover that even a serious commitment to this kind of maturity (perfection) is inadequate to produce fulfillment. No human being has the power to constantly and consistently live at this level, fulfilling these instructions from the Master. Nevertheless, as a believer I do know there is a way the Lord's instruction can become a reality in my life. How? Through the power provided by the heavenly Father in His Holy Spirit because, *"The fruit of the Spirit is love" (Galatians 5:22).* Relying on this God-given power and living daily with a heartfelt commitment to be like Jesus, as disciples of Christ we discover it is possible to live the teaching of God's Son, Who said, *"You therefore must be perfect, as your heavenly Father is perfect" (5:48).* We also discover the significant role this godly love plays in developing a productive Christian life.

THE GUIDING PRINCIPLES FOR THE PRODUCTIVE CHRISTIAN

6:1-34

CHAPTER 25

6:1-4 ... Practice Genuine Generosity

"Beware of practicing your righteousness before other people in order to be seen by them, for then you will have no reward from your Father who is in heaven.

"Thus, when you give to the needy, sound no trumpet before you, as the hypocrites do in the synagogues and in the streets, that they may be praised by others. Truly, I say to you, they have received their reward. But when you give to the needy, do not let your left hand know what your right hand is doing, so that your giving may be in secret. And your Father who sees in secret, will reward you."

Parades may be held for a variety of reasons. However, one primary motivation undergirds every parade...the desire of the participants to be seen and honored by others. If no one stood on the parade route to acknowledge the skill, beauty, gifts, goals, or accomplishments of the participants the parade would be cancelled. Parade participants want attention; they like attention; they deliberately put forth effort to draw that attention. Such activity and motivation is normal and acceptable in the world, but not in God's kingdom.

Jesus began the next section of the Sermon on the Mount *(6:1-18)* with a two-sentence summary warning kingdom people about piety parades. He then addressed three specific areas of kingdom living where such parades might occur...giving, praying, and fasting.

Of special interest is the fact that the Master did not instruct citizens of His kingdom about the need to give, pray or fast. His teaching was based upon the assumption that these would be normal activities in kingdom life. Rather than the 'doing' of these activities He focused upon the possibility of such actions being driven by inappropriate motivation - *"When you give - pray - fast..." (6:2,5,16)... "to be seen" (6:1), "[to] be praised by others" (6:2).*

Therefore, Jesus warned His followers to guard against bringing their earthly parade attitudes into kingdom life. To emphasize that warning the Master alerted His disciples to several important truths, using giving to the needy as His first illustration.

He began by announcing God does not automatically reward people who perform obvious acts of righteousness *(6:1)*. Certainly, it seems logical that one who does righteous deeds, especially the ones expected by God, would receive the Almighty's blessing. Jesus, however, declared that, even a kind and generous deed will not receive the only reward that counts - God's reward - when done for the wrong reason. The Master clearly indicated God is not a rich philanthropist who drops wonderful rewards on people simply because they have performed a good deed, such as giving to the needy.

Why? Because the reason for their action does make a difference. One who gives to *"be praised by others"* should expect nothing beyond man's recognition *(6:2)*. In that recognition *"they have received their reward"* for their 'righteous' action. Nothing more will be given.

We feel safe in stating that few followers of Jesus give out of a motivation to hear someone say, "There goes a spiritual Christian," or "Isn't their generosity wonderful?" However, a longing for people-approval can show its presence in other ways. If a kingdom person thinks, "There was not a single word of appreciation expressed for what I gave," are they not saying, "I want man's approval"? Does such thinking suggest they have just participated in a piety parade? Jesus tells His followers, "Don't worry about people's recognition, approval, or appreciation. That is not important. It is God's blessing that should concern you."

The Lord also addressed a second, more subtle kind of human recognition...self recognition. He used an interesting illustration of *"your left hand [knowing] what your right hand is doing" (6:3).* Jesus' words paint an interesting picture in our minds...the left hand reaching across to pat the right hand and declaring, "You just did a wonderful thing; your giving was so generous."

What does such a picture represent? Self congratulating self. It is possible for Christian people to keep their own spiritual ledger where *"practicing...righteousness" (6:1)* is recorded so they can express inward self-praise for having established a profit margin of good works. Praising one's self for 'doing such good thing' is as much a piety parade as seeking the praise of others. The Master cautions, "Just as you should avoid performing good deeds to impress others, avoid the trap of self-congratulations. Stay out of all piety parades."

Interestingly, Jesus did not suggest it is wrong to desire approval or rewards. To the contrary, His instruction clearly indicates the need to seek God's approval, and He speaks openly of receiving God's reward *(6:4).* To want God's recognition and reward is a legitimate motivation. Scripture often encourages kingdom people by speaking of God's reward in a positive manner.

"Henceforth there is laid up for me the crown of righteousness which the Lord...will award to me on that Day" (2 Timothy 4:8); "Knowing that from the Lord you will receive the inheritance as your reward" (Colossians 3:24); "Rendering service...as to the Lord not to man, knowing that whatever good anyone does, this he will receive back from the Lord" (Ephesians 6:7,8).

As a kingdom person I can look forward to being given a reward. Obtaining that reward is a legitimate desire, and I will receive God's reward if I serve out of love and seek only His approval. However, the Master has cautioned me, *"[I] will have no reward from [my] Father who is in heaven" (6:1)* if I get caught up in piety parades.

CHAPTER 26

6:5-8 … Maintain an Effective Prayer Life

"And when you pray, do not be like the hypocrites. For they love to stand and pray in the synagogues and at the street corners, that they may be seen by others. Truly, I say to you, they have received their reward. But when you pray, go into your room and shut the door and pray to your Father who is in secret. And your Father who sees in secret, will reward you.

"And when you pray, do not heap up empty phrases as the Gentiles do, for they think that they will be heard for their many words. Do not be like them, for your Father knows what you need before you ask him."

Giving - Praying - Fasting. All are acts of *"righteousness" (6:1)* which become a natural part of the kingdom person's life. However, Jesus alerted His followers to the possibility that even these actions can be built on a faulty foundation. Having addressed that issue with giving the Master offered additional instruction specifically related to the practice of prayer.

The Lord's teaching about prayer can be summarized quite simply...all prayers are not equal; some are acceptable to God and some are not. He told His followers there is a right way to pray and a wrong way to pray. The Master explained the errors to avoid *(6:5-8)* and provided a pattern to follow *(6:9-13)*. Heeding His instruction results in the heavenly Father acknowledging and hearing the kingdom person's prayers.

Jesus reminded kingdom people of two important truths regarding their communication with God. In keeping with the basis *(6:1)* for His comments in this section of the Sermon on the Mount *(6:1-18)* the Lord reminds His listeners again that when praying Christians should not be concerned with impressing the people around them. The foolishness of that concern is easily illustrated. Imagine that while experiencing a personal visit with the Queen of England your attention was not focused on the Queen, but upon what ordinary people observing your visit thought about you personally. Foolish? Yes. It is even more foolish to be concerned about what human beings think of you when you are talking with the God of the universe.

Jesus understood the nature of the human heart and saw that even when approaching God in prayer we can let our concern about the attitudes of men overwhelm us. Such a concern reveals that while we supposedly are praying to God in reality the focus can be on self. When kingdom people pray the reactions of people around them should not be a matter of any concern. If they are, Jesus declares, those reactions will be the only benefit the pray-er receives from that prayer *(6:5)*.

The Master also cautioned kingdom people about trying to impress God with the words they use. It is a worldly attitude, He explained, that thinks a prayer requires *"empty phrases" (6:7)* - many words, repetition and correct terminology - to get God's attention. Kingdom pray-ers don't need to impress God and, furthermore, cannot impress God! Therefore, Jesus instructed them to reject the temptation of using words for that purpose. Followers of Jesus wrapped in the Beatitudes would not struggle with this temptation because they are fully aware of their own spiritual bankruptcy *(5:3)* and are motivated to act out of a pure heart *(5:8)*.

With these words Jesus explained to citizens of His kingdom that the reactions of other people and the need for impressive terminology should not be matters of concern when they pray. When communicating with the heavenly Father disciples need to focus all attention on God. The mind should be centered in God and the intent should be to glorify God.

The Master also explained to kingdom people how this can be accomplished. The key, He indicated, is isolation. Get away from anything that might interfere with your 'God-focus.' He instructed believers, *"Go into your room and shut the door and pray to your Father" (6:6)*.

Jesus not only taught the prayer principle of isolation, He practiced it. Scripture tells us the Lord *"went out to a desolate place, and there he prayed" (Mark 1:35)*, and He *"would withdraw to desolate places and pray" (Luke 5:16)*. [Scripture shows us that other men of God also understood and practiced the 'isolation principle' *(Daniel 6:10; Acts 10:9)*.]

Four words from Jesus' instruction provide the protection against empty praying and lead to fruitful praying...*"pray to your Father" (6:6)*. Prayer is communication with God. As with an effective telephone conversation productive praying is the result of total focus on the person at the other end of the line. A kingdom person completely centered on God will receive the Father's full attention and the reward of answered prayer.

Eliminating concern about the reactions of other people and focusing totally upon God will wrap my motivation in sincerity *(6:5)*. Because the listener is my *"Father"* I need not worry about eloquence. He understands me personally so my prayer can be packaged in simplicity *(6:7)*. This can be effectively accomplished by uttering my prayer in quiet solitude *(6:6)*. When I address these three issues as Jesus instructed I will experience the joy of serenity, knowing that the *"Father...will reward [me]" (6:6)*, providing exactly what I need because the *"Father knows what [I] need before [I] ask him" (6:8)*.

CHAPTER 27

6:9-13 ... Follow the Prayer Pattern

~

"Pray then like this: 'Our Father in heaven, hallowed be your name. Your kingdom come, your will be done, on earth as it is in heaven. Give us this day our daily bread, and forgive us our debts, as we also have forgiven our debtors. And lead us not into temptation, but deliver us from evil.'"

Having explained to His followers what they should not focus on when praying *(6:5-8)*, Jesus proceeded to give a pattern prayer which re-directed their focus away from other people and self. In the Lord's model prayer He revealed a focus directed primarily on God. He showed us God's acceptance: *"Our"*; God's Love: *"Father"*; God's Home: *"in Heaven"*; God's Holiness: *"hallowed be your name"*; God's Objective: *"Your kingdom come"*; God's Desire: *"your will be done"*; God's Pattern: *"on earth as it is in heaven"*; God's Generosity: *"Give us this day"*; God's Provision: *"our daily bread"*; God's Mercy: *"and forgive us our debts"*; God's Expectation: *"as we also have forgiven our debtors"*; God's Guidance: *"And lead us not into temptation"*; God's

Protection: *"but deliver us from evil."* [In the common ending to this prayer - God's Reign: 'For Yours is the kingdom'; God's Capability: 'and the power'; God's Majesty: 'and the glory'; God's Timeline: 'forever'; all followed by the kingdom person's acceptance: 'Amen' (So be it).]

Often overlooked in discussions about the Lord's model prayer is this complete focus on God. It is all about a glorious and magnificent God, His kingdom, and His people. Its purpose is to glorify and honor God. According to the Master Himself He answers this or any other prayer for the purpose of glorifying the name of God *(John 14:13).* So, it is not surprising to see that once the Master focused on the role and nature of God *(6:9)* He then described how to pray about God's kingdom.

Careful examination also reveals a natural progression in this model prayer *(6:10)* - *"Your kingdom come"* speaks of the ultimate goal; *"Your will be done"* explains the way by which the kingdom of God becomes a reality; *"on earth as it is in heaven"* shows the pattern to follow when doing God's will. It is interesting to note that these requests differ greatly from the usual requests expressed by kingdom people...good health, material abundance, trouble-free living. For disciples of Jesus the desire for the establishment and growth of God's kingdom should precede and supersede any and all desires related to their personal lives.

Jesus also included the life of the kingdom person in the model prayer. In speaking first of their present life - *"Give us this day our daily bread" (6:11)* - the Lord gave a picture of daily and continued dependence upon God. All kingdom people know that *"Every good and every perfect gift is from above" (James 1:17)*, but one's socioeconomic situation may make it more obvious to some than to others. Poverty stricken Christians may experience a greater spiritual blessing than those living in the midst of material abundance simply because they are forced to trust God's promises for their necessary provisions *(6:33)*. They truly understand the meaning of praying for their daily bread.

In addition to the present Jesus also addressed the past life of kingdom people: *"Forgive us our debts, as we also have forgiven our debtors" (6:12)*. Every living person faces a significant problem... the debt they created with God through their failure to give Him the allegiance, loyalty, and service He is owed. Nothing a human being has can adequately repay this debt. Only God's forgiveness can remove it from the ledger.

Fortunately, a loving and forgiving God *(Nehemiah 9:17)* has made provision in Jesus Christ for addressing this problem: *"[Jesus] is the atoning sacrifice for our sins" (I John 2:2) [NIV]*. The kingdom person can experience continued forgiveness of this debt by uttering the plea described by the apostle John *(1 John 1:9)*. Interestingly, in the model prayer the Master described a basis for that plea: *"as we also have forgiven our debtors."* It appears that Jesus realized this prerequisite might puzzle kingdom people because He provided an amplified explanation of it in the verses following this pattern prayer *(6:14-15)*.

Having dealt with both past and present issues the Lord looked into the future of a kingdom person's life, addressing still another significant need. *"Lead us not into temptation, but deliver us from evil" (6:13)*. Jesus knew every person faces a twin-threat enemy...the first threat - *"temptation"* - being interior *(James 1:14)* and the second - *"evil"* - being exterior *(1 Peter 5:8)*. These two threats, when coupled, create a force resulting in severe spiritual problems for the follower of Jesus; problems that can be life altering and destroying. Without protection the kingdom person faces an extremely precarious situation.

Fortunately, in this prayer the Lord assured His disciples the needed guidance and protection is available. The apostle Paul further amplified this assurance when he explained that God's Holy Spirit is the source of a kingdom person's strength and power against both Satan and the desires of carnal flesh *(Romans 8:5-17)*.

In summary, the model prayer provided by the Master shows me the wonderful blessing that results from praying with complete attention focused on God, being filled with desire for the coming of His kingdom and the perfect fulfillment of His will on earth as it is in heaven. In addition, understanding more completely the content and meaning of the Lord's model prayer and praying with a sincere heart *(6:5-8)* I also experience provision for present daily needs (from God the Father), forgiveness for my past failures (through Jesus Christ, the Son), and protection for my future (by the Holy Spirit). In following this prayer pattern I discover that it contributes significantly to my productive Christian life.

CHAPTER 28

6:14-15 ... Express a Forgiving Spirit

~

"For if you forgive others their trespasses, your heavenly Father will also forgive you, but if you do not forgive others their trespasses, neither will your Father forgive your trespasses."

Having completed His instruction regarding the kingdom person's prayer life Jesus selected from His pattern prayer the petition regarding forgiveness *(6:12)* and undergirded it with an expanded explanation *(6:14-15)*.

Why did the Lord choose forgiveness as the topic for emphasis? Why not focus on the idea of God as Father? That was certainly a new concept to many people of His day. Or the kingdom issue? This held great interest in the minds of the Jews. Or praying for daily bread? Many of His hearers would have seen that as a major concern. Why did Jesus select the forgiveness issue?

Even a surface perusal of the life of Jesus reveals the importance of forgiveness in His own practice and teaching. Before healing a paralytic Jesus forgave the man's sins *(Luke 5:20)*. To the woman who poured perfume on His feet He declared, *"Your sins are forgiven" (Luke 7:48)*. The Master explained the purpose of His own death as being *"for the forgiveness of sins" (Matthew 26:28)*, and He clearly instructed His disciples to proclaim the message of *"repentance and forgiveness of sins"* throughout the entire world *(Luke 24:47)*. Jesus knew His holy Father could not connect with a sin-stained soul, so forgiveness with its removal of guilt was essential for any person seeking to experience fellowship with God.

True disciples of Jesus Christ would have no problem understanding the importance Jesus placed on God's forgiveness of their past sins and the continuing need for the forgiveness of present and future sins. But would they understand the need for demonstrating a forgiving spirit toward their own offenders? What better way for Jesus to get their attention and stress the importance of forgiveness in the life of His followers than to couple God's forgiveness of their own sin with their willingness to forgive those who offended them.

Perhaps the Master also emphasized this matter so kingdom people would recognize the need for consistency in their lives as Christ-ians. Surely, disciples of Jesus could understand the simple logic of being willing to give to others what they wanted to receive for themselves. This expectation was not unique to forgiveness. In the Beatitudes the Lord coupled giving and receiving mercy *(5:7)*, and later in this Sermon connected the kind of judgment they displayed toward others to the judgment they would receive personally *(7:1-2)*. Undoubtedly Jesus wanted a follower of His to recognize that consistency in one's life is fundamental to effectively shining their light before an inconsistent and sin-darkened world *(5:16)*.

Maybe the Lord gave special emphasis to forgiveness because He knew that people often struggle with the mere thought of forgiving. Even committed followers of Jesus Christ can find it extremely challenging to demonstrate a forgiving spirit.

Forgiveness is neither just nor fair. It requires the offended person to bear the burden. They must be willing to personally absorb the offense...suffer the loss. They cannot retaliate or get even. Therefore, to forgive is to agree to come out on the short end in the present circumstance. However, by connecting forgiveness between people with forgiveness from God it becomes clear that this short end is only apparent and temporary. In reality, the kingdom person who is a forgiver always comes out ahead. First, as Jesus clearly stated, it undergirds their assurance of forgiveness from the Father *(6:14)*. In addition, through this forgiving spirit the Christian closely conforms to the image of Christ *(Romans 8:29)*.

Jesus also knew that the act of forgiving would protect His followers from the threat of spiritual self-destruction. An unforgiving spirit creates an inner issue that only goes deeper and leads to bigger problems. The writer of Hebrews described a *"root of bitterness [that] springs up and causes trouble, and by it many become defiled" (Hebrews 12:15)*. Such is the unforgiving spirit. It develops a root of bitterness in the heart, growing a plant of negative issues which then produces sour fruit that touches and often ruins many lives. By imitating their forgiving heavenly Father *(Ephesians 4:32-5:1)* a kingdom person establishes protection from the root of bitterness and the fruit of selfishness. The Lord knew He was showing His followers how to avoid a vengeful and destructive spirit that would handcuff them with resentment and hate, destroying the effectiveness of their witness.

Just as no Christian virtue may be more challenging than forgiveness it is possible that no Christian virtue more effectively demonstrates a Christlike and godly spirit. True forgiveness is so unique and so seldom seen that its presence attracts the world's attention. When people in that world see the impact of this good deed at work in my life, some will be led to praise the Father in heaven *(5:16)*...and that should be the ultimate goal of my forgiving spirit.

CHAPTER 29

6:16-18 ... Develop Heartfelt Devotion

"And when you fast, do not look gloomy like the hypocrites, for they disfigure their faces that their fasting may be seen by others. Truly, I say to you, they have received their reward. But when you fast, anoint your head and wash your face, that your fasting may not be seen by others but by your Father who is in secret. And your Father who sees in secret, will reward you."

Upon completing His extended comments on prayer and forgiveness Jesus returned to His original instruction *(6:1)*, this time focusing on fasting as an illustration. In essence the Master declares, "When fasting don't draw attention to yourselves. Rather, act normally *("Anoint your head and wash your face" - 6:17)*. Fasting has a higher purpose than self-aggrandizement."

Many Scripture texts mention fasting and provide enlightenment regarding its purpose. [David *(2 Samuel 12)*, King Jehoshaphat *(2 Chronicles 20)*, Ezra *(Ezra 8, 10)*, Queen Esther *(Esther 4)*, Daniel *(Daniel 9)*, the city of Nineveh *(Jonah 3)*, Saul/Paul *(Acts 9)*, Antioch church *(Acts 13)*, Paul & Barnabas *(Acts 14)*, and Jesus *(Matthew 4)*.] These references reveal that fasting connects with specific attitudes and significant events in the lives of God's people. Fasting's association with repentance, sorrow, seeking God's will, desire for special help from God, and preparing for special or demanding efforts indicates it is not merely some casual religious practice. To the contrary, fasting - almost always associated with prayer - plays a vital role in the lives of kingdom people seeking a closer relationship with God.

As with many issues, even in the disciple's spiritual life, some may ask, "What do I get out of fasting?" This question reveals a basic misunderstanding regarding the purpose of fasting. Through Zechariah God specifically confronted the Jews about this attitude: *"When you fasted and mourned...was it for me that you fasted?" (Zechariah 7:5)*. Even though a 'faster' will benefit spiritually from this practice the primary goal is not self-centered, but God-centered. Fasting helps provide an environment in which a disciple can concentrate totally on God.

Many people temporarily omit eating in order to focus fully on some important activity. College students, for example, sometimes eliminate meals so they can devote all attention to studying for a final exam or completing a class project. In such instances the objective is seen to be so important that nothing, including the basic necessities of life, can be allowed to interrupt or interfere.

So it is with fasting in the life of God's children. They choose to deliberately set everything aside, including food, in order to focus attention without interruption or interference upon God and the things of God. The objective may be seeking God's will, God's wisdom, God's power, God's help, or restoring a broken or weakened relationship with God through repentance and sorrow for sin.

Through fasting God's servant offers a strong declaration of intention: "Nothing is more important to me at this time than fellowship and communion with God. I am focusing totally on the Father and the issue at hand. Therefore, I am eliminating anything and everything that might interfere with that relationship. I will allow nothing, including food, to come between me and God." This becomes a demonstration of loving God with all of one's heart, soul, mind, and body *(Mark 12:30)*. In a very real sense the 'faster' responds to Paul's appeal, *"Present your bodies as a living sacrifice, holy and acceptable to God which is your spiritual worship" (Romans 12:1)*.

Understanding this helps to clarify the reason why Jesus warned His followers against fasting in a way that draws attention to one's self. A fasting servant cannot seek to impress people and reach out to God at the same time. The Father rewards the fasting kingdom person only when the heart, mind, soul and body are focused on Him alone *(6:17-18)*.

Having absorbed Jesus' instruction about fasting perhaps a related issue also needs to be considered - its current relevance. Little is said about this practice among modern believers. Probably not one in one thousand gives fasting more than a passing thought, with even fewer having experienced it. So, is this teaching of Jesus irrelevant for today's disciples?

Perhaps a different kind of questioning gives us much needed direction regarding this matter in our spiritual lives. What blessings are we missing by not including time devoted totally to God? What could God really do in our lives if we developed a willingness to set aside every worldly barrier, including food, so we could focus totally on Him for a given period of time? What failures are we experiencing due to an absence of in-depth involvement in this beneficial and fruitful spiritual experience?

Fasting carries no magical power to change my life. However, when there is such a devotion to and hunger for God in my heart that I set aside everything, including the basics of life, am I not opening up the channels for God's Holy Spirit to work in and through me with power I have never before experienced? With all worldly hinderances set aside will not this passion for God lead me to enjoy a spiritual walk unavailable through other means? How would my life be changed if I placed fasting side-by-side with giving and praying, as Jesus did in this part of His message *(6:2,5,16)*?

After addressing fasting as if it would be a common practice in the lives of kingdom people, the Master assured His followers, *"When you fast..."* with your focus totally on God *"...your Father, who sees in secret will reward you." (6:18).*

CHAPTER 30

6:19-21 … Establish A Clear Life Objective

~

"Do not lay up for yourselves treasures on earth, where moth and rust destroy and where thieves break in and steal, but lay up for yourselves treasures in heaven, where neither moth nor rust destroys and where thieves do not break in and steal. For where your treasure is, there your heart will be also."

These words of Jesus though easy to understand may be some of the most challenging to obey. One person observed, "As far as most of us are concerned, these verses might just as well not be in the Bible. We believe Jesus spoke them. We believe they are divinely inspired. But we do not think they apply to us. We do not obey them. So far as we are concerned, it is the same as if the Lord never spoke them."

"Do not lay up for yourselves treasures on earth" (6:19) is not a difficult statement to comprehend. There are no unknown terms or nebulous phrases in this instruction. The Master's teaching is clear

and uncomplicated, so why do His followers experience such a great challenge in obeying Him?

God's most faithful saints, being earthly beings like everyone around them, continually use the things of this earth. Some of those things are fundamental to life, while others can be considered extras or luxuries. However, Jesus explained that all of these earthly treasures have a common characteristic - they are subject to decay and destruction, and all can be taken away. Because people understand this fact they try to collect and protect earthly treasures in many ways, including the use of preservatives, alarms, and a variety of safe havens. None of these efforts guarantees protection, and even if they did the ultimate result cannot be changed. The day will come when *"the first heaven and the first earth [have] passed away" (Revelation 21:1).*

Even though they understand the truth of Jesus' words God's kingdom people often struggle to obey this teaching. Why? Firstly, like much of the teaching in the Lord's instruction to His followers, the message of these verses is in direct conflict with the worldly standards bombarding believers every day. From every direction, through every type of modern media available, the call comes to gather and hold the treasures of earth. The world tells God's children, as it does everyone else, that earthly things are vitally important because they will provide the happiness and security everyone desires. This continual external pressure on believers makes that call difficult to resist.

However, Jesus used two words in His instruction that reveal a second problem, an internal problem. It may be of greater significance than the call of the world to gather its earthly treasure. The phrase, "*...for yourselves...*," addresses the issue of a self-centered spirit still active in the believer's heart. These words reach into the core of one's being, challenging the most basic motivations and revealing that the kingdom person has not fully denied self as Jesus instructed at another time *(Mark 8:34).*

This problem, putting self and the treasures of the world ahead of Christ, is not unique to twenty-first century Christians. Seeing believers of his day focused on self as revealed by their attitude toward things of the world, Paul saw the necessity of urging the Colossian saints to, *"Set [their] minds on things that are above, not on things that are on earth" (Colossians 3:2)*...instruction still relevant for today's believers.

Serious thinking kingdom people confronted with this reality begin to realize that chasing after the world's treasures is not unlike a skilled brain surgeon spending his time collecting band-aids. Nonetheless, even with this awareness Christ's disciples still face the attraction of earthly treasure and struggle to find a solution to the problem.

Having high-lighted the problem in a negative statement - *"Do not lay up..."* - the Lord provided the solution via a positive statement - *"But lay up for yourselves treasures in heaven..." (6:20).* He proposed a common process found many places in Scripture...replace the negative action with a positive action *(Romans 6:19; Ephesians 4:22,24; Colossians 3:5,12).* Because of the fundamental difference between earthly treasures and heavenly treasures one cannot be storing up both at the same time. A disciple, by taking the positive action, automatically eliminates the negative action.

What are these heavenly treasures about which Jesus speaks? Paul told Timothy to *"Instruct [believers]...to do good, to be rich in good works, to be generous, willing to share,"* indicating that in this way they will be *"storing up for themselves a good foundation for the age to come" (1 Timothy 6:18-19) [NKJV].* Perhaps Paul was aware of Jesus' words to the rich young ruler, "*...give to the poor, and you will have treasure in heaven*" *(Matthew 19:21)*, or His similar words as recorded by Luke: "*Sell your possessions, and give to the needy. Provide yourselves with moneybags that do not grow old, with a treasure in the heavens that does not fail...*" *(Luke 12:33)*. Clearly, these are some of the "*good*" treasures produced in the believers' lives as a result of their Christ-like actions.

After identifying the problem and explaining the solution Jesus wraps up this instruction with what appears to be merely a simple statement of fact: "*For where your treasure is, there your heart will be also*" *(6:21)*. However, this fact comes alive within my heart to serve as a driving force, compelling me, as one seeking to follow Jesus' instruction, to willingly take the action *(6:20)* which will motivate my heart appropriately. From now on, as one who has "*been raised with Christ,*" my clear objective in life is to "*seek the things [treasures] that are above*" *(Colossians 3:1)*.

CHAPTER 31

6:22-23 … Focus Attention in the Right Place

~

"The eye is the lamp of the body. So if your eye is healthy, your whole body will be full of light, but if your eye is bad, your whole body will be full of darkness. If then the light in you is darkness, how great is that darkness!"

Jesus followed His instruction to *"lay up for yourselves treasures in heaven" (6:20)* with three specific steps that will lead to the fulfillment of those words in the kingdom person's life. The Lord first told His followers to focus their attention in the right place *(6:22-23)*. Then He taught them to center their activity in the right place *(6:24)*. Finally, Jesus explained the need to anchor their trust in the right place *(6:25-34)*.

The Master Teacher's first step addressed a fundamental principle of life: *"The eye is the lamp of the body" (6:22a)*. We can understand the point of this object lesson through personal experience. Our eye serves as an instrument through which the brain obtains information. Having received that information our brain then selects an objective for our journey and sends commands to our body so the objective can be reached. The eye's effectiveness in gathering information for our brain is determined by the amount and nature of available light. Light is vital because it alone provides illumination necessary for our eye to see. In the absence of light the darkness makes it impossible for our brain to process adequate information in order to focus on the right objective.

Jesus used this illustration to help His followers understand that the treasures they store up, whether earthly or heavenly, will be determined by the focus-point of their spiritual eye. In essence the Lord declared, "Where you keep the eye of your attention and understanding focused will determine, more than anything else, whether you get earthly or heavenly treasures." Therefore, He explained, keeping one's eye narrowly focused on the right place, the light of God, allows it to permeate the believer's whole being *(6:22b)*, thus equipping him to seek the right objective, *"treasures in heaven."*

Translators have described the *"eye"* as good, clear, pure, and healthy. However, the most descriptive concept may be the one which says, *"If therefore thine eye be single…" [KJV].*

A *"single"* eye is an undivided eye, and its meaning is clarified through the common phrase 'undivided attention.' With this word Jesus stressed the need to focus undivided attention upon the light of God. A disciple who gives undivided attention to the light of God experiences heavenly things flooding their earthly life. When every decision and action is made in the light of relevant eternal spiritual values the kingdom person also consistently stores up treasures in heaven.

Interestingly, the Master Teacher changed His description when addressing the contrasting circumstance. The opposite of 'single' as used in His earlier statement would be 'divided'. However, He replaced that idea with *"bad"*. If the focus is *"bad"* the result will be severe spiritual darkness *(6:23)*. [*"Bad"* comes from the same word translated *"evil"* in *6:13*.] This eye with improper focus is not just a divided eye, it is an evil eye that leads to being filled with great darkness. Paul associated this darkness with *"the power of Satan" (Acts 26:18)*.

What is the result of this *"great...darkness"* about which Jesus spoke? Paul also enlightens us regarding this matter: *"They are darkened in their understanding, alienated from the life of God..." (Ephesians 4:18)*. John tells us this kind of person *"does not know where he is going, because the darkness has blinded his eyes" (1 John 2:11)*. The words of an Old Testament prophet describe the problem faced by these spiritually blinded people: *"They do not know the thoughts of the Lord; they do not understand his plan" (Micah 4:12)*.

A bad spiritual eye does not let in spiritual light, so the soul is left to grope in great darkness when confronted with spiritual issues. This condition leads to a complete distortion of spiritual reality, including calling good bad, and bad good. Light and darkness are also reversed *(Isaiah 5:20)*. That which ought to be rejected is accepted *(1 Corinthians 2:14)*. Because the *"eye"* - attention - is focused away from the light the darkness of the world blinds the heart and it becomes impossible to be sensitive to spiritual concerns. The inevitable result causes the darkened heart to think the treasures of earth represent all that is important.

Again, the message of Jesus is clear and simple. There are only two ways for me to look at everything in the world - through eyes focused singly on the light of God or through eyes that are blinded by darkness. The first will give me clear spiritual vision, making it possible to discern and understand the issues of life in a way never before comprehended. The second produces spiritual blindness, double vision or shadowy vision filled with images that are dim, flickering and unclear, leading to values that will pull me away from God. The Master's teaching is plain. In order to seek spiritual heavenly treasures and enjoy a productive Christian life I must keep my attention focused solely on the light of God...and that light is Jesus Christ *(John 8:12; 12:46).*

CHAPTER 32

6:24 ... Center Activity in the Right Place

~

"No one can serve two masters, for either he will hate the one and love the other, or he will be devoted to the one and despise the other. You cannot serve God and money."

These may be among the most sobering and soul-searching words Jesus ever spoke. The Master Teacher emphasized one of His strongest teachings with one three-syllable word, seven two-syllable words, and twenty-eight one-syllable words. These words, simple though they are, drill to the core of a kingdom person's life and deposit a powerful challenge: "Choose to serve only one master."

"No one..." - The Lord stated a universal principle. No person can hear His words and conclude, "This does not apply to me." Jesus said there are no exceptions. Not a single individual escapes the thrust of the truth He was about to deliver.

"...can serve two masters..." - The New English Bible, in changing just one word, gives a better translation: *"...can be the slave of*

two masters." A slave is owned by the master, whereas a servant may work as an employee. The "*slave*" word brings to mind the kingdom person's relationship to the Supreme Master as often mentioned by the Apostle Paul. When writing to the Roman Christians he used the same terminology, providing additional explanation regarding this "*slave*" status. The Apostle's description helps us understand why in our kingdom life it is impossible to be a slave of two masters *(Romans 6:16-18)*. Those masters described by Paul are diametrically opposed - "*sin*" vs "*righteousness*".

"*Either...or...*" - In keeping with the pattern He established in the previous verses *(6:22-23)* Jesus explained there are only two options - focusing our attention either on light or on darkness. In words yet to be spoken in the Sermon on the Mount, as well as in future teaching, the Lord returned several times to this 'either-or' proposal *(7:13-14; 24-27; 10:32; 12:30, 35; John 3:16-20; 5:29)*. Clearly, the Master considered all of life to be a matter of choosing between two options. For the follower of Jesus it is always "*either...or.*"

"*...cannot...*" - Jesus avoided the nebulous 'perhaps...maybe...if' used so often by an uncertain world. He did not suggest that serving two masters is unadvisable or difficult. Rather, Christ stated with clarity, it is not possible. This principle appears throughout Jesus' teaching in a variety of forms *(Matthew 10:37-38)*. The total commitment required by the Lord made serving two masters both logistically and spiritually impossible.

"*...serve...*" - Jesus' previous instruction *(6:22-23)* addressed the need to focus one's attention in the right place, an inward matter involving the spirit, mind and soul. Now *(v. 24)* He moves to the disciple's use of his body. Paul addressed this same issue when he described using "*the parts of your body*" as either "*instruments of wickedness*" or "*righteousness*" *(Romans 6:13) [NIV]*. Like the Master, the Apostle announced the activity of one's life - serving - can only be used for one of two diametrically opposed purposes *("either-or")*. The activity - service - of a kingdom person's life can be offered to only one master.

"...money..." - At first glance this seems like a strange twist of terminology. Why did Jesus not say one cannot serve both God and Satan, or the world, or self? Why did He unexpectedly bring a physical, materialistic item into this revelation of spiritual truth? It was Jesus' habit to use practicalities in teaching. Everyone of His six antitheses *(5:21-48)* addressed practical circumstances of life. The Lord's teaching always addressed the 'so-what' question by relating the spiritual truth to real-life situations. Nothing is more real-life than money. In the cultures of Jesus' day, as in ours, money or its equivalent was life's number one issue. It was the one object for which everyone worked. It touched and was vital to almost every area of life. Therefore, it became the primary area of focus, as it has in cultures of all ages. So, in the context of the Lord's teaching *"money"* represented that to which people of the world devoted their life's service. Life was primarily about either getting or using money and all that it represented. Jesus said no one, especially His servants, can center their service on both the money for which the world searches and God. It is one or the other.

A summary paraphrase of Jesus' words in this verse might read: "I'm going to give you a universal principle that applies to everyone without exception. You cannot be owned and controlled by two masters at the same time. Because only one can be the controller that of necessity eliminates the other. If you choose to serve the first as the center of your activity then you automatically eliminate the second and vice versa. It is impossible for the activity of your life to be centered at the same time on serving God and serving the world, including what that world considers to be the primary necessity of life - money. Therefore, you must make a choice between these two options regarding the center of your life's activity."

Contrary to the likes of the world Jesus described a totalitarian relationship. Service cannot be partly here and partly there. It is an all or nothing choice. As a believing Christian the focus of my attention *(6:22-23)* and the center of my activity *(v.24)* can be in only one place. I must choose whom I will serve. The Master teaches with clarity that He expects complete loyalty, total allegiance, and single-hearted commitment in my service to Him.

CHAPTER 33

6:25-34 ... Anchor Trust in the Right Place

~

"Therefore I tell you, do not be anxious about your life, what you will eat or what you will drink, nor about your body, what you will put on. Is not life more than food, and the body more than clothing? Look at the birds of the air: they neither sow nor reap nor gather into barns, and yet your heavenly Father feeds them. Are you not of more value than they? And which of you by being anxious can add a single hour to his span of life? And why are you anxious about clothing? Consider the lilies of the field, how they grow: they neither toil nor spin, yet I tell you, even Solomon in all his glory was not arrayed like one of these. But if God so clothes the grass of the field, which today is alive and tomorrow is thrown into the oven, will he not much more clothe you, O you of little faith? Therefore do not be anxious, saying, 'What shall we eat?' or 'What shall we drink?' or 'What shall we wear?' For the Gentiles seek after all these things, and your heavenly Father knows that you need them all. But seek first the kingdom of God and his righteousness, and all these things will be added to you.

"Therefore do not be anxious for tomorrow, for tomorrow will be anxious for itself. Sufficient for the day is its own trouble."

Human beings, including God's children, have a great natural ability to picture the worst long before it happens, if ever. With little effort we imagine situations that turn our best efforts into our biggest problems. We become experts at 'what-if' reasoning. "What if I focus my attention on God and center my service in Him and bad things happen?" Overwhelmed by imaginary mental images, we allow the 'what-ifs' to become excuses for not following the Lord's instruction.

Jesus knew the human mind would respond to His words about serving God *(6:24)* with 'what-if' thinking. So, He offered instruction regarding the process for confronting this mindset His way. With the precision of an effective attorney arguing a life or death case the Lord offered significant reasons why kingdom people should rely on the faithfulness of their heavenly Father *(6:32-33)*. Knowing that He offered a foundation of strong arguments supporting His instruction, the Master stated forcefully, *"Do not be anxious" (6:31,34)*. Simply put, His words declared, "Just as you have focused your attention in the right place, and you have centered your activity in the right place, now I'm telling you to anchor your trust in the right place."

The Master Teacher began laying the foundation for this forceful instruction with four illustrations from nature. He first argued from the greater to the lesser...life vs. things that support life *(6:25)*. God is the source of life. If God is the source of life itself, it seems only logical that He would also provide the things of lesser importance that are necessary to support His gift of life. Why would the Creator give life, but not provide that which is needed to sustain it?

In offering His second illustration Jesus reversed the procedure, arguing from the lesser to the greater...birds vs. humans *(6:26).* Birds do not have the value of human beings. They have no soul. Christ did not die for the salvation of birds. Surely, Jesus indicated, if the Father takes care of the lesser (birds) will He not also take care of the greater (humans) for whom His Son died? It would make no sense to carefully watch over soulless beings that live only a short time while ignoring beings with souls that will live for eternity.

The third illustration from nature grows out of an inherent weakness in every human being. Even though humans enjoy the greatest gift, God-given life, and stand at the top of all God's creation there is one thing they cannot do...change the nature of life *(6:27).* Mankind, especially modern mankind, likes to believe he is in control and can eventually extend life forever. However, the Master reminded His followers their anxiety about life never changes the fact that they cannot think themselves into a longer existence. Eventually, human death is a certainty, so it is not productive in any way to worry about the 'what-ifs' of living or dying.

Flowers became Jesus' final illustration from nature *(6:28-30).* The beauty of flowers exceeds the splendor of Scripture's richest king, Solomon. So the Lord argued, "If the hand of God decorates short-lived stems with magnificent beauty, won't that same God excel even more in His provision for the needs faced by long-lived human beings?" Flowers soon wither and die, but people are eternal.

The Master Teacher proceeded to lay the next block in His foundation for that forceful command - *"do not be anxious"* - by turning to the spiritual realm. He explained that when God's children devote their attention and energy primarily to the affairs of the world they put themselves in the same category as unbelievers *(6:32).* In so doing, they adopt the world's value system and become immersed in the world's lifestyle. This behavior contradicts everything Jesus taught previously in this Sermon - His followers are different in attitudes, in character, and in actions. How unreasonable and unworthy it is for a Christ-ian to approach life's challenges in the same way as a non-Christ-ian.

The world-centered lifestyle of unbelievers contradicts all that is inherent in the believers' claim about Almighty God. When followers of Jesus approached life with the same attitude as unbelievers they became like the pagans who saw their gods as aloof, uninterested, and unconcerned about the well-being of their subjects. In speaking of *"your heavenly Father" (6:26,32)* Jesus reminded His followers of this unique connection kingdom people have with the God of the universe. To follow the unbeliever's lifestyle minimizes that special relationship and denies the nature of the God believers claim to honor.

Furthermore, in following the pagans' worldly life-style emphasizing self-preservation a kingdom person ignores the personal compassion and caring concern of their heavenly Father for each individual. At another time Jesus told His followers the spiritual Father will treat them better than they are treated by their own earthly Fathers *(Luke 11:11-13)*. Jesus reminded believers God knows what is happening in the life of each of His children, evidenced in *"even the hairs of your head [being] numbered" (Matthew 10:30)*. So, why should disciples of Jesus live as if God does not know or care what is going on in their life? Why should they act as if the responsibility for life itself is totally on their own shoulders?

The Master's final foundation stone is wrapped in a combination of life experience and common sense. Life has taught every Christian that the current day will bring many issues, both expected and unexpected, which will keep them engaged in the immediate moment of the here and now *(6:34)*. So, why should believers increase that burden by becoming immersed in the 'what-ifs' of tomorrow? What a waste of physical, emotional, mental and spiritual energy to worry about that which has not yet happened. Jesus said this kind of behavior demonstrates only one thing - *"little faith" (6:30)*.

With illustrations from nature, the need for spiritual consistency, and simple common sense Jesus built a strong foundation for His forceful instruction: *"Do not be anxious" (6:31,34)*. He tells us quite simply, "Throw out your what-ifs." The Master teaches me to not only focus my attention on God *(6:22-23)* and to center my activity around God *(6:24)*, but also to anchor my trust in God *(6:25-34)*. Such trust finds powerful reinforcement in the assurance given to me by the Apostle Paul, *"My God will supply every need of yours according to his riches in glory in Christ Jesus" (Philippians 4:19)*.

CHAPTER 34

6:33 … Submit Everything to a Single Priority

~

"But seek first the kingdom of God and his righteousness,
and all these things will be added to you."

Jesus began this part of the Sermon on the Mount declaring that His disciples should store up heavenly rather than earthly treasures *(6:19-21)*. He named three steps that would lead to this objective - focus attention on the light of God *(6:22-23)*, center activity in service to God *(6:24)*, anchor trust completely in God *(6:25-34)*. A kingdom person might respond asking, "What practical process can I follow that will accomplish this on a daily basis?" A single sentence included in Jesus' description of the final step provides the answer.

"But seek first his kingdom and his righteousness and all these things will be added to you" (6:33). One word summarizes the instruction contained in Jesus' statement...prioritize. Proper application of this priority principle will lead to success in accomplishing the three steps the Lord gave for storing up treasures in heaven.

The Master's priority principle begins with an active, continuous process...*"seek."* Unfortunately, some followers of Jesus want all God's blessings without any seeking on their part. They seem to think the words of a great song, "Fill my cup, Lord," eliminate their own responsibility. However, no passive 'fill my cup' concept is taught anywhere in Scripture. The New Testament overflows with action instructions. It is a continual and diligent seeking that the Lord expects from His disciples. No kingdom person will ever reach a point in this life where they can quit seeking, claiming to have accomplished ultimate success in obtaining the desired heavenly treasures. Even the Apostle Paul realized this truth *(Philippians 3:13-14).*

What should the Master's follower continually seek? The Lord clearly identified the specific objective...*"the kingdom of God and his righteousness."*

The word *"kingdom"* brings different thoughts to different people. Some think of the Old Testament kingdom of Israel which was temporarily headed by earthly kings such as David and Solomon. Others identify the kingdom with the church. Still others believe there is a kingdom yet to be established when Jesus returns.

Perhaps a completely different concept fits the context of this message from Jesus. One only needs two things to establish a kingdom...first, a king who rules; second, subjects who acknowledge that king and submit to his authority. Applying this simple idea to the teaching at hand produces a circumstance where the kingdom of God becomes reality in a person's life when they acknowledge the Lord as King and willingly submit to His authority. Is this not what Jesus described when He later declared, *"the kingdom of God is within you" (Luke 17:21) [NIV]*? If so, the Master is telling us to continually seek and maintain a submissive relationship before God.

The Lord did not stop with 'kingdom seeking.' He also instructed His followers to seek *"righteousness,"* which is addressed three ways in Scripture. First, there is the declared righteousness Paul described through the illustration of Abraham's life. It is a righteousness credited to Abraham because in faith he believed *(Romans 4:3,9)* and later acted upon God's promises *(James 2:21-22)*. Paul explained that *"God will credit* [declare] *righteousness—-for us who believe in him who raised Jesus our Lord from the dead" (Romans 4:24) [NIV]*.

A second righteousness had already been described by the Lord in an earlier part of the Sermon on the Mount...heart righteousness *(5:20)*. He explained that the righteousness of His followers must exceed that of legalistic religious leaders who focused only on performing every act of life precisely according to their definition of correctness. Jesus contrasted this with the heart righteousness He expected from His disciples in their attitude toward people *(5:21-26)*, inward purity *(5:27-30)*, loyalty *(5:31-32)*, integrity *(5:33-37)*, reactions *(5:38-42)*, and perfect love *(5:43-48)*.

We turn again to Paul's writing to the Roman Christians for the description of the third righteousness...works righteousness *(Romans 6:13,19)*. The Apostle clearly explains that, in fact, righteousness does include external actions. When a believer who has been declared righteous functions out of a righteous heart the result will be observable righteous works. These Christlike actions give evidence that God's Holy Spirit is present in this life, the life of a person who has sought the kingdom of God.

Finally, we address the key word in this instruction, the priority principle word...*"first."* Jesus indicated that the seeking activity He described must be the number one concern of a kingdom person's life.

Unfortunately, many believers do not always give the top position in their lives to God's kingdom and righteousness. They may seek God's kingdom and God's righteousness, but not first. Controlling priority is given to what they eat, what house they want to buy, which clothes they prefer to wear or what self-satisfying experiences they want to enjoy. Later they will seek the things of God providing this does not create too much upheaval in other priorities. The Master's teaching makes this unacceptable behavior. He declared that seeking the things of God must be the number one priority for a kingdom person.

As a result of following the Master's priority principle I will enjoy the special promise that God always provides for those who put Him first... *"all these things will be added to you" (6:33b).* Focusing my eyes on God first, centering my activity in serving God first, anchoring my trust in God first will not only bring to me the assurance that this life's needs will be provided by God, it will also assure that I am storing up treasures in heaven as I walk the path of productive Christian living on this earth.

THE PROTECTION FOR THE PRODUCTIVE CHRISTIAN

7:1-27

Be Committed to Life-Building Habits

CHAPTER 35

7:1-5 ... Examine Self First

~

"Judge not, that you be not judged. For with the judgment you pronounce you will be judged, and with the measure you use it will be measured to you. Why do you see the speck that is in your brother's eye, but do not notice the log that is in your own eye? Or, how can you say to your brother, 'Let me take the speck out of your eye,' when there is the log in your own eye? You hypocrite, first take the log out of your own eye, and then you will see clearly to take the speck out of your brother's eye."

How would you react if a friend of yours convinced his next-door neighbor to leave town for a few days so he could have a secret affair with that neighbor's wife? What would be your response toward a co-worker who, under pressure, denied even knowing a person who was, in fact, his best friend? What thoughts would enter your mind if you saw a church family stand before the congregation and openly lie about the size of their contribution to a church financial campaign?

Before you explain your feelings in each of these situations read the words of Jesus in this text *(7:1-5)*. How should a kingdom person apply these words to his own heart and mind in reacting to these people and their behavior? [Undoubtedly, you recognized the people described here as modern illustrations of Biblical characters: King David *(2 Samuel 11)*, the Apostle Peter *(Luke 22)*, Ananias and Sapphira *(Acts 5)*.]

Some people would tell us there should be no reaction. They wave their flag of disapproval anytime someone denounces inappropriate or sinful behavior, rejects questionable or false ideas, or shows a negative reaction toward another's attitudes. These 'objectors,' quoting the words of Jesus *(7:1)*, would have everyone think that it is never appropriate to speak negatively of someone else's actions, attitudes, or beliefs.

However, Jesus did not issue a command for kingdom people to suspend their mental faculties, ignore wrong-doing, or refuse to discern between good and evil or truth and error. In fact, the words Jesus spoke at other times demonstrate this 'eliminate judgment' approach is not a proper application of His instruction. For example, He also declared, *"Do not judge by appearances, but judge with right judgment" (John 7:24)*. Likewise, the Apostle John supports the need for judgment applied appropriately: *"Test the spirits to see whether they are from God" (1 John 4:1)*. Paul not only declared that he had already judged one guilty of inappropriate behavior, but instructed Corinthian Christians it was their responsibility to do so within the church, leaving judgment of those in the world to God *(1 Corinthians 5:1-3, 12-13)*.

What then is the proper application of this instruction from Jesus? The Master described specifically the intended recipient for this teaching. He spoke to that person who is quick to pass judgment upon *"the speck in [his] brother's eye,"* yet does *"not notice the log in [his] own eye" (7:3)*. The problem Jesus identifies is not one of passing judgment on inappropriate attitudes, actions or behavior. The problem is one of chronological priority. The Master does not issue a direct command to avoid all judging. Rather, He insists that the right order be followed. "Before you address someone else's issues," the Lord says, "first address your own." According to Jesus, failure to do this turns the accuser into a *"hypocrite."* Prior to examining the failures and short-comings of another person the 'judger' must *"first take the log out of [his] own eye."* To do that *"the log"* must be identified.

Did Jesus intend for the word *"log"* to be understood generally, covering any weakness in the accuser's life, or did He have something more specific in mind? Most people have interpreted that *"log"* to be referencing either the accuser's own shortcomings that are similar to the failure being judged, or any shortcoming in general that might be present in the life of the 'judger.'

Is it not possible, however, that Jesus was referring to a specific fault?...one being demonstrated in this very act of judging? Could the *"log"* in the accuser's eye be the *"log"* of self-righteousness? Regardless of what other failures might be present, the one that now drives the accuser is the feeling that they are positioned to be sitting in judgment over the life of another. At least subconsciously, the accuser has concluded that their own life is sufficiently righteous to be pointing out the unrighteousness in the life of their brother. They seem to be sharing in the attitude of the Pharisee who declared, *"I thank you that I am not like other men" (Luke 18:11)*.

Is Jesus specifically warning us to be sure there is no spirit of self-righteousness present when we look upon the attitudes and actions of other disciples? According to His instruction failure to do so can quickly turn us into hypocrites.

The Lord always treated hypocrites harshly. He showed them no mercy, held them up for derision, ridiculed and condemned them *(Matthew 23)*. Certainly, no one is more guilty of hypocrisy than believers who insist others maintain a sin-free lifestyle while at the same time ignoring inappropriate attitudes or actions in their own lives, especially their own self-righteousness. Remembering that God hates the emptiness of hypocrisy should lead every disciple to exercise judgment with great care.

In addressing hypocritical self-righteousness and lack of self-examination Jesus reminded the person who is quick to judge others, "[Don't forget] *you will be judged" (7:2)*. Ultimately, judgment confronts everyone... *"It is appointed for man to die once, and after that comes judgment" (Hebrews 9:27)*. Later in His ministry the Master stated, *"the Son of Man...will repay each person according to what he has done" (Matthew 16:27)*, describing that time of judgment to be faced by all. Peter also reminded believers they *"call on him as Father who judges impartially according to each one's deeds" (1 Peter 1:17)*. Kingdom people who acknowledge a day is coming when they will personally face God's judgment will be motivated to focus on self-examination more than judgmental examination of others.

It is also noteworthy that in the act of passing judgment a person reveals they believe there is a standard to be followed. Therefore, Jesus stated, that person will be judged against their own standard *(7:2)*. They will be measured with the same critique and precision they apply to the person who is the object of their judgment. [This is called the Law of Reciprocity - what you give determines what is given back to you.] Is not this the kind of impartiality Peter mentioned when describing the Father's action *(1 Peter 1:17)*? Believers, being aware of the standards to be applied in their own future judgment, will think carefully before quickly and critically passing judgment upon the attitudes and actions of others.

Contrary to common belief Jesus in this teaching did not tell His followers to completely eliminate passing judgment on others. The Lord did not declare, "Ignore the speck in the other person's eye, and don't take any action when they express ungodly attitudes or practice acts of sin in their life." He simply said, "Get the order right...do the self-examination and self-correction first." Following this process will equip a disciple to judge properly *(7:5b)*. Having experienced their own piercing and sincere self-examination, the believer, now filled with humility *(Matthew 5:3)*, meekness *(5:5)*, mercy *(5:7)*, and a pure heart *(5:8)* will be prepared to kindly assist others.

Paul speaks of that approach when he informs kingdom people, *"If anyone is caught in any transgression, you who are spiritual should restore him in a spirit of gentleness" (Galatians 6:1)*. What will make me, as a follower of Jesus Christ, the kind of Christian who is spiritually prepared to address another person about the speck in their eye? I must first examine my own life and address my own shortcomings, especially the spirit of self-righteousness. Having followed the instructions of my Master - "Be sure to do your self-examination and self-correction first" - I am then spiritually prepared to gently help my brother/sister in the family of God address their weaknesses.

CHAPTER 36

7:6 ... Respect Sacred Things

~

"Do not give dogs what is holy, and do not throw your pearls before pigs, lest they trample them underfoot and turn to attack you."

If you have ever wondered why, on the night of His trial and crucifixion, Jesus responded to Pilate's question but refused to say a word to Herod *(Luke 23:3,9)* you might find the answer in these two sentences from the Sermon on the Mount. These words also provide insight for direction the Lord gave His disciples at a later time in His ministry when He told them to *"shake off the dust from your feet"* and leave town *(Matthew 10:14)*. They further explain Paul's response when he turned away from some of the people in Antioch *(Acts 13:50-51)* and Corinth *(Acts 18:5-6)*.

An important distinction exists between the instruction the Master gave in the preceding verses *(7:1-5)* and the application of this verse *(7:6)*. Previously, He described the appropriate way to deal with issues in a *"brother's" (7:3)* life. Now Jesus speaks of people whom He compares to *"dogs"* and *"pigs."* Clearly these descriptions identify two different kinds of persons. This undoubtedly grabbed the attention of the Lord's listeners.

Dogs in Jesus' day were not pampered, cuddled and treated like family members as in modern American society. To the contrary, they were semi-wild animals often traveling in packs as dirty scavengers. People considered them dangerous because dogs were sometimes vicious and diseased. These were animals to be avoided. Therefore, with this description Jesus' hearers knew he was declaring there were some people whom His disciples should avoid.

Pigs had even lower status than dogs in the society of Jesus' day. They were looked upon as the epitome of uncleanness and considered an abomination by the Jews because of instruction in the Mosaic Law. So strong was this feeling that when a pagan leader entered the Jerusalem temple, sacrificed a pig on the altar, and forced the priests to eat pig-meat it produced a Jewish uprising known historically as the Maccabean Revolt. Any Jew in Jesus' crowd would conclude that the Master Teacher had just identified people who should be rejected by the Lord's followers.

No one who heard Jesus' words could possibly misunderstand His point. Whereas He previously taught about the need for cautious judgment toward others, now the Lord indicates the opposite truth. There are some people in the world toward whom the kingdom person should exercise strong judgment. Even though followers of Jesus should not act as supercritical judges of their brothers-in-error, neither are they to act as simpletons who blindly accept everyone regardless of their actions or attitudes. Kingdom people should not pretend everyone thinks and acts with the same sincere motivation. While some hearers will heed God's message and some will neglect or reject it, there are also people who will seek to undermine and destroy it, even attempting to eliminate the messengers who proclaim God's word.

Jesus gave His messengers special instruction regarding the delivery of God's truth to these people described as *"dogs"* and *"pigs."* "Remember, the message you are delivering to the world is *'holy,'"* the Lord tells His followers, "and likened in value to *'pearls.'"*

In short, Jesus told His disciples to make a judgment; recognize that not everyone will receive teaching and testimony regarding the Lord Jesus Christ with openness or respect. Some people in the world will not only reject it, but will react like vicious scavengers controlled by the desire to destroy that which is *"holy."* Others, if given the opportunity, will trample deliberately upon God's precious *"pearls."* Therefore, the Lord instructed His followers to carefully evaluate the situation before laying God's eternal word out to be treated as meaningless drivel.

It is true that the Master instructed His followers to preach and teach His good news throughout the world *(Matthew 28:18-20; Mark 16:15-16; Luke 24:46-47; Acts 1:8)*. However, in this Sermon on the Mount teaching He also declared that there are mockers and revilers who will berate, trample upon and seek to destroy God's divine message in all of its richness and truth. The Lord Jesus Christ plainly instructed kingdom people not to waste time nor to dishonor the sacredness of God's message by laying it before such people.

It may conflict with today's popular political correctness, even held by some in the church, but according to the Master there are specific situations where I, as a representative of the Lord Jesus Christ, should not waste time laying out God's sacred pearls before the *"pigs"* and the *"dogs."*

CHAPTER 37

7:7-11 … Rely on Dependable Support

~

"Ask, and it will be given to you; seek, and you will find; knock, and it will be opened to you. For everyone who asks receives, and the one who seeks finds, and to the one who knocks it will be opened. Or which one of you, if his son asks him for bread, will give him a stone? Or if he asks for a fish, will give him a serpent? If you then, who are evil, know how to give good gifts to your children, how much more will your Father who is in heaven give good things to those who ask him!"

Any sensible follower of Jesus, upon carefully reading and seriously considering His teachings to this point in the Sermon on the Mount, will declare with heartfelt concern, "I can't! I can't! I can't! There is no way I can live like this...follow these principles...obey Jesus' instruction. It is way beyond my ability!" That disciple would be one-hundred percent correct. Not even a deeply sincere Christian is equipped with the necessary innate ability to successfully follow these teachings from the Master. Perhaps that is why the Lord chose this place in His teaching to give a most assuring promise.

Jesus knew this instruction was beyond every disciple's ability to fulfill. From a human perspective the challenge was overwhelming. At this point, with hearers potentially feeling a sense of utter hopelessness, He offered a special promise. "God stands ready to empower kingdom people who want to live the Christlike lifestyle victoriously. Help is on the way."

Three times the Lord gave an unequivocal declaration, *"It WILL be given....You WILL find...It WILL be opened" (7:7,8).* We are reminded of comparable words, recorded by the Apostle Paul many years later, which seem to build upon and expand these promises from Jesus, *"God is able to make all grace abound to you, so that in all things at all times, having all that you need, you will abound in every good work" (2 Corinthians 9:8) [NIV].*

Precious as each reassurance is, God's servants cannot ignore the required action Jesus placed before each of the promises: *"Ask... seek...knock."* He gave these not as options to be considered, but as prerequisites to the fulfillment of the promises. Interestingly, the intensity grows with each succeeding required activity.

The first action commanded by the Lord - *"Ask"* - immediately directs our thinking to prayer. When explaining the need for them to be fruitful and productive in their kingdom living Jesus told His followers, *"Ask whatever you wish, and it will be done for you" (John 15:7).* The Apostle John guaranteed believers that when they prayed *"according to his will"* God would hear their prayers, assuring that they would have *"the requests that [they] have asked of him" (1 John 5:14-15).* Prayer is the first step for a disciple of the Lord who wants to successfully apply in his own life the Master's teaching from the Sermon on the Mount. God is waiting to hear the believer's voice because He wants to help that disciple become everything Jesus'

Sermon describes. God does not want you to fail; He wants you to succeed in your quest to live the productive Christian life.

To *"ask"* identifies the need, but the next step - *"seek"* - requires more extensive personal effort and involvement. A person who is seeking leaves no stone unturned in their effort to find the desired object. A seeking kingdom person will search for every possible opportunity to apply the truths Jesus gave to His followers in this message. That disciple, instead of standing idly by waiting for opportunities to come his way, will *"seek"* diligently for the means of accomplishing the fulfillment of each godly principle laid out by our Lord.

An old saying summarizes these first two commands very well. Pray (*"ask"*) as if everything depended upon God, and work (*"seek"*) as if everything depended upon you.

However, the Lord Jesus followed His instruction to *"ask"* and *"seek"* with a third command - *"knock"* - demonstrating the need for intensified persistence in seeking God's blessing. Parents who discovered their six-year old missing from the backyard would ask every person in sight, "Have you seen my child?" Additionally, those parents would seek for their child in every nearby building and behind every bush and fence in the neighborhood. Having no success in finding the child, they would intensify their efforts by going to every house in the community, knocking on every door as they continued asking and seeking until the child was found. This is the kind of process Jesus mapped out for kingdom people to follow in their daily goal to experience divine empowerment for effectively fulfilling the Master's instruction.

As followers of the Lord Jesus we enjoy days of ecstasy living at the top of God's mountain, but we also experience walks through the deepest of valleys. Regardless of which scenario we experience the instruction remains the same…*"ask - seek - knock"*…and do so with the assurance that positive results will come.

Jesus reinforced His commands with the promises that *"it WILL be given...you WILL find...it WILL be opened" (7:7-8),* and illustrated these words with a real-life example every parent within His hearing would understand *(7:9-11).* At the heart of normal parenting is the never ending desire to help one's child in every possible way. The Lord reminded His listeners that the natural instinct of a loving parent always responds positively to a child expressing its needs. The love and concern in the heart of God for His children far exceeds that of an earthly parent. Therefore, disciples of Jesus should easily understand that active asking, seeking, and knocking are guaranteed to bring a positive response from their heavenly Father.

This assurance given by the Master of the kingdom encourages each of us in our effort to follow His teaching. No matter how great the difficulty any part of Jesus' instruction may seem every child in God's family can see it successfully fulfilled in their own life. Doubters and naysayers cannot be comfortable in God's kingdom because there is no place for their 'I can't' syndrome. With this promise from the Lord of the kingdom planted deeply in my heart I, as a kingdom citizen, am empowered to stand tall and confidently proclaim with Paul, *"I can do all things through him who strengthens me" (Philippians 4:13). "Ask - Seek - Knock"* and I will walk the path of a productive Christian life.

CHAPTER 38

7:12 ... Let One Life-Principle Control Everything You Do

~

"So whatever you wish that others would do to you, do also to them, for this is the Law and the Prophets."

Most people who know the content of this text as the Golden Rule are aware that it is a general principal similarly taught by many of history's religious leaders and philosophers. However, closer examination of this principle as given by Jesus Christ in the Sermon on the Mount reveals a specific application for people who make Him the Lord of their lives.

Our Master gave special emphasis to the uniqueness as well as the significance of this instruction when He declared "*this is the Law and the Prophets.*" Every word found in the Law or proclaimed by the Prophets in regard to interpersonal relationships is summarized by this simple teaching. All New Testament instruction for believers is also capsulized in these words, making them a concise guideline by which the kingdom person can be sure their conduct is godly.

This Golden Rule as taught by Jesus declares, "Always make yourself and your actions beneficial to others in the same way you would want their actions to be beneficial to you." It has been called, "the topmost peak of social ethics" and "the Mount Everest of all ethical teaching." For Christians it is the simplest way both to understand and express a Christlike spirit. In applying this principle to their lives, believers experience the reality of Paul's words - *"be conformed to the image of His son" (Romans 8:29).*

As believers, we sometimes hear conflicting instruction regarding how to connect our Christian life to all of the people around us. One person says, "Do it this way," while another equally sincere individual declares, "No, do it that way." At the same time the disciple's inner voice may be saying, "I think I ought to do it differently than either of those ways." Thankfully, the Lord's Golden Rule resolves this conflict by showing the confused follower of Christ exactly how to address this real-life situation...do it the way you would want it done to you.

By serving as the ultimate standard this principle helps us evaluate all other standards. Often we look at our own standards and consider them to be straight as an arrow. However, when compared to this principle given by the Lord the crookedness of our own guidelines becomes readily apparent. It forces us to confront the self-centeredness of our life...how focused we are on our own needs, cares, loves, joys and dreams. We are reminded of our natural tendency to want everything, first and foremost, to contribute to our own well-being. Now, in the Golden Rule Jesus instructs us to transfer the focus of that generous self-interest to the other person, seeking to do for them what we would normally do to produce blessings for ourselves.

Paul, without mentioning these words from the Master, provided the same instruction when he wrote, *"Do nothing from rivalry or conceit, but in humility count others more significant than yourselves. Let each of you look not only to his own interests, but also to the interests of others. Have this mind among yourselves, which is yours in Christ Jesus" (Philippians 2:3-5).*

Kingdom people do not live by this principle because it is utilitarian, because it is productive or because it pays. Sometimes none of these describes the result of following this instruction. God's children choose to live by this Golden Rule because it is the clear teaching of our Master and the supreme ethical standard for all who are part of God's kingdom.

As Jesus said in beginning His statement, this principle applies to *"whatever."* However, Jesus' Golden-Rule-teaching also can be applied specifically for the purpose of fine-tuning all of His instruction in the Sermon on the Mount. Most of His teaching in this message addresses issues in a general way without detailed instruction. For example, the Lord says His followers are to love their enemies *(5:44)*, but does not say how to do it. He tells kingdom people to be reconciled to their brothers *(5:24)*, to practice forthright integrity *(5:37)*, to *"give to the needy" (6:3)*, and to *"forgive others their trespasses" (6:14)*. He gives no precise guidelines describing the way to accomplish any of these. The Golden Rule fills that void. When obeying any instruction given by their Master followers of Jesus should always do it for the purpose of impacting others in the same way they would want to be impacted.

The Golden Rule also refines the teaching of New Testament writers. Paul said a spiritual follower of Jesus who sees a brother *"caught in any transgression"* should care enough *"to restore him in a spirit of gentleness" (Galatians 6:1).* But how? The Master said, *"Whatever you wish that others would do to you, do also to them."*

The apostle instructed each Ephesian Christian to *"speak the truth with his neighbor" (Ephesians 4:25).* Even kingdom people can speak truth in a cutting and hurtful way. However, that will not happen if the believer follows the Lord's instruction to, *"Do to others what you would have them do to you."*

The power of our Lord's Golden Rule is beyond imagination. Proper application of this principle to life's day-to-day situations could completely revolutionize one's personal relationships with family, friends, fellow-Christians, and even one's spiritual opponents. It summarizes everything taught by the Law, the Prophets, our Master, and His apostles. It fine-tunes for kingdom people the application of all New Testament instructions as they are applied to daily, real-life situations.

With this one statement Jesus settled a thousand difficult points and eliminated the need for volumes of additional instruction. In every way, at every time, in every circumstance this principle of Christian discipleship identifies the way Jesus wants me to live. Shaping my obedience in everything Christ taught, the Golden Rule guides me and all other kingdom persons into living the way our Master wants us to live. In this Mount Everest of all ethical teachings our Lord gave me a standard by which I can and God will measure my conduct.

Be Alert to Life-Threatening Dangers

CHAPTER 39

7:13-14 ... Choose the Right Associates

"Enter by the narrow gate. For the gate is wide and the way is broad that leads to destruction, and those who enter it are many. For the gate is narrow and the way is hard that leads to life, and those who find it are few."

Throughout the Sermon on the Mount Jesus presented a challenging lifestyle for people who would be His disciples, never suggesting the life of a kingdom person would be easy. In approaching the conclusion, the Master provided a unique twist to His instruction. Unlike a salesman whose assurance would be, "Everyone wants this product," Jesus declared the opposite: "Very few people will decide to travel through life on the path I have described." He explained this development through the use of four contrasts...the narrow road vs. the broad road; the narrow/small gate vs. the wide gate; the destination *"that leads to life"* vs. the destination *"that leads to destruction,"* and the *"few"* who travel one road vs. the *"many"* who travel the other.

People of the world often use the derisive terms 'narrow' and 'narrow-minded' in an attempt to categorize followers of Jesus Christ, their beliefs and their lifestyle negatively. Very few persons throwing out those terms realize they were upstaged by the Lord Himself when He openly described His road as *"hard"* with a *"narrow gate"* at its end. Kingdom people can respond with a simple but truthful rebuttal statement when someone casts that supposedly negative accusation: "You are right…*"narrow"*…is the exact term Jesus Himself used to describe His way of living; you are in complete agreement with the Lord on that one."

Most people who accuse Christians of narrowness are suggesting this description does not fit the broadminded Jesus they picture in their own minds. They might be shocked if they understood fully Jesus' own assessment of His role and His teaching regarding this matter. For example, Christ Himself presented an extremely narrow declaration when He said, *"I am the way, and the truth, and the life. No one comes to the Father except through me" (John 14:6).*

Those who had been with Jesus clearly understood this narrow path the Master described. The apostle John stated, *"Everyone who…does not abide in the teaching of Christ, does not have God" (2 John 9).* Peter, a highly esteemed apostle by both his compatriots and believers of many centuries, spoke plainly, *"And there is salvation in no one else* [meaning Jesus], *for there is no other name under heaven given among men by which we must be saved" (Acts 4:12).* The apostle Paul added his declaration writing, *"For there is one God, and there is one mediator between God and men, the man Christ Jesus" (1 Timothy 2:5).*

Why is *"narrow"* a fitting description of 'King Jesus Highway #1'? Among other reasons, His highway is *"narrow"* because travelers are told specifically what they must believe *(John 3:18)*, it allows for only one master over a person's life...Jesus Christ *(Matthew 10:34-39)*, and it requires complete denial of self *(Mark 8:34-35)*.

Considering the narrowness of the King's highway, we should not be surprised to know that very few, in comparison to the *"many"* on the world's highway, will be traveling with Jesus and arriving with Him at the destination. At every point in His teaching the Lord clearly indicated those who accept His instruction and faithfully follow him to the end represent a very small part of the population. Plainly and simply the Master Teacher stated only the *"few"* will enjoy the life He provides, but there will be "many" who travel the road and enter the gate *"that leads to destruction."*

Anyone listening to or reading these words of Jesus faces a clearcut choice regarding the road they decide to travel. According to the Lord there are only two possibilities...one leads to life, the other leads to destruction. Obviously, Jesus wanted His listeners to understand they had a choice between two very distinct and very different destinations. There can be little question regarding His desire that travelers choose to walk the road with Him because He issued a simple invitation: *"Enter by the narrow gate."*

His words reveal that the Master wants me to arise each morning and declare, "I am a follower of Jesus Christ and a child of God. I am a citizen of God's kingdom, and my desire is to live at the top of God's mountain. Therefore, I will not walk on the broad road with the majority of people in this world. I choose to walk on the Master's road which He described as *'narrow.'* My guide is the Lord Jesus Christ, my Master, my Savior. I surrender everything to follow Him. Therefore, I will choose my associates carefully. Other citizens of the Lord's kingdom will be my traveling companions and we will honor, obey and serve our Lord. I have decided to follow Jesus. I am walking the path to productive Christian living."

CHAPTER 40

7:15-20 ... Reject False Teachers

"Beware of false prophets, who come to you in sheep's clothing, but inwardly are ravenous wolves. You will recognize them by their fruits. Are grapes gathered from thornbushes, or figs from thistles? So, every healthy tree bears good fruit, but the diseased tree bears bad fruit. A healthy tree cannot bear bad fruit, nor can a diseased tree bear good fruit. Every tree that does not bear good fruit is cut down and thrown into the fire. Thus, you will recognize them by their fruits."

Our examination of the Sermon on the Mount has clearly revealed the obvious contrast between the teaching of Jesus Christ and the beliefs, philosophies, and practices of the modern world. Today's world declares, "Absolute truth is non-existent. What I believe is as true as what you believe; we should be completely tolerant of each other's beliefs because no one is 'more right' than anyone else." All of Jesus' instruction stands against these ideas, so He sounds an alarm in this text clearly identifying the danger.

The Master's warning - *"Beware of false prophets" (7:15a)* - revealed two simple but important truths. First, an objective standard of truth, does in fact, already exist. The presence of that which is false necessitates the pre-existence of that which is truth. Therefore, in order to follow the Lord's instruction regarding *"false prophets"* people needed to know who or what represented that pre-existent truth.

John called Jesus, *"The true light" (John 1:9)*, and declared that He came into this world *"full of grace and truth" (John 1:14)*. The apostle based this instruction upon the bold announcement Jesus made regarding Himself: *"I am the way, and the truth, and the life" (John 14:6)*. The Master is the objective standard of truth. Therefore, a kingdom person can know that any prophet presenting a message in conflict with Jesus or His teaching is one of the *"false prophets."*

The second truth in Jesus' simple statement addressed the need for His disciples to be alert regarding people who proclaim that which is not truth *(7:15a)*. The Lord's followers must be cautious at all times because, He warned, people delivering false teaching will sometimes be deceivers who appear to have good motives. In reality, they are malicious destroyers ...*"ravenous wolves" (7:15b)*. In the natural world animals and even people who look good can sometimes be dangerous. Likewise, in the spiritual world teachers who look good and sound good may, nevertheless, be a perilous threat to the welfare of believers.

Such people do not come wearing signs announcing, "I'm a ferocious wolf not good for your spiritual health." In fact, the opposite is true. The Master warned these teachers may come *"in sheep's clothing" (7:15b)*, appearing to be sincere kingdom people. They look right; they talk right; they act right. No one suspects them of wrong-doing or maliciousness, but in reality they are poisonous to the flock of God.

Adding to their threat, these *"false prophets"* in *"sheep's clothing"* do not attack from outside the flock. They become part of the kingdom crowd and work from inside. Paul described the situation to Ephesian Christians, *"Even from among your own number men will arise and distort the truth in order to draw away disciples after them,"* and added, *"So be on your guard" (Acts 20:30-31) [NIV]*. The apostle Peter also warned, *"there will be false teachers among you, who will secretly bring in destructive heresies, even denying the Master" (2 Peter 2:1)*.

Christians who are neglectful in study of God's word, lazy in their prayer life, and careless about the things of God can easily be deceived by these *"false prophets"* who are pleasant, positive and sometimes very knowledgeable. They succeed as counterfeits because of their ability to look and sound like the real thing. According to Jesus kingdom people must remember that even though they may walk like sheep, sound like sheep and look like sheep, in reality these teachers are wolves *"in sheep's clothing."*

How can God's family identify these 'false prophet' wolves? Jesus told His followers, *"you will recognize them by their fruits" (7:16, 20)*. Why look at their fruit? Because *"a diseased tree"* does not produce *"good fruit" (7:18)*. Ultimately their true nature will be revealed.

That which is of God is special...unlike anything else in this world. The Lord's teachings stand alone; nothing equals them. The lifestyle described by Jesus is different. The kind of person the Master pictured in the Beatitudes and the kind of behavior He proposed in the rest of the Sermon on the Mount can only be called unique. *"False prophets"* will eventually violate this uniqueness, demonstrating they are not Beatitude people and do not live or teach the truths of the Sermon on the Mount or other teachings from the Master. Their lack of Christ-likeness will become evident.

Jesus revealed their true standing with God when He warned of the false teachers' ultimate destiny, declaring that a tree producing bad fruit *"is cut down and thrown into the fire" (7:19)*. Peter said they bring *"upon themselves swift destruction" (2 Peter 2:1)*. Therefore, kingdom people must be alert always, never joining in partnership with these counterfeits.

The world may proclaim there is no such thing as absolute truth and that it does not make any difference what one believes. However, the Master Teacher - Himself the truth and the proclaimer of God's truth - warned His followers that not everyone speaks, teaches or lives the truth. He further cautioned that some of those people who deliberately seek to draw us away from the truth will attempt to do their malicious work inside the church. So, He told Christians who want to live a productive Christian life to be always on guard...*"Beware of false prophets."*

CHAPTER 41

7:21-23 ... Guard Against Empty Self-Confidence

"Not everyone who says to me, 'Lord, Lord,' will enter the kingdom of heaven, but the one who does the will of my Father who is in heaven. On that day many will say to me, 'Lord, Lord, did we not prophesy in your name and cast out demons in your name, and do many mighty works in your name?' And then will I declare to them, 'I never knew you; depart from me, you workers of lawlessness.'"

Early in the Sermon on the Mount Jesus told His followers *"unless your righteousness exceeds that of the scribes and Pharisees, you will never enter the kingdom of heaven"* *(5:20)*. Surely, having heard Jesus' contrast of the two kinds of righteousness through the six antitheses *(5:21-48)* and His additional explanations of kingdom life-style righteousness *(6:1-7:5)*, the Lord's audience must have developed some understanding of the difference between the righteousness of their Jewish leaders and the righteousness described by the Master.

The distinction between the Pharisee's righteousness and that of Jesus could not be more obvious. The leaders of the Jews focused on avoiding the wrong acts and performing the right ones. Murder, adultery, oath-taking, giving, praying, fasting...all were among the acts discussed by the teachers of the Law. Certainly, these kinds of actions needed to be considered. However, Jesus' teaching revealed that the Pharisees chose to ignore the primary issue of concern related to these matters.

The Master addressed that neglected issue time and again throughout the Sermon on the Mount. He stressed the absolute necessity of a right attitude, right spirit and right motive behind the right action. The Lord did not disparage the actions addressed by the Jewish teachers, but He did attack their failure to include the necessary righteous, God-glorifying, servanthood motives driving those actions. The teachers of religion heralded their own connection with the Almighty, using their religious actions as proof, even though they omitted the vital connecting force required for true fellowship with God. In reality, as false practitioners of their religion, their self-confident sense of spiritual security was empty and meaningless.

Having revealed that unholy circumstance in a variety of situations, Jesus alerted His own disciples regarding the potential for the same development in their lives. The Master's listeners heard Him give a frightening warning...a warning that applied to those who thought they were walking the *"narrow"* way *(7:14)*. The Lord described the real possibility of people believing they were His faithful followers yet, in reality, being totally disconnected from fellowship with Him.

The Master's description focused on persons who truly believed they were His committed servants. They spoke the right word in describing Him...*"Lord, Lord" (7:21)*. In that they were correct: Jesus Christ is Lord. The apostle Peter proclaimed, *"God has made him [Jesus] both Lord and Christ" (Acts 2:36)*. These people claiming to be His followers could not have been more accurate in their description of Jesus.

Those confident 'followers' involved themselves in the right activities...prophesying, driving out demons, performing miracles. These were things done by both Jesus and some of His disciples *(Acts 4:30)*. The people here described by the Lord announced they also were practitioners of such actions *(7:22)* and, it is important to note, the Master did not dispute their claim.

Perhaps the most outstanding characteristic of the people described by Jesus was their claim to practice all of their activity *"in your [Jesus'] name" (7:22)*. Again, it is significant that the Lord did not accuse them of misspeaking.

Surely, if anyone could be regarded as sincere and secure followers of Jesus these people described by Christ could claim that position. They talked right; they did the right things; they credited the right Person. Unfortunately, the Master Teacher laid out a frightening pronouncement over them: *"I never knew you" (7:23)*. He did not say they were in error, did the wrong things, or made inaccurate claims. Rather, the Lord announced there had never been a connection between these people and Himself. To the contrary, He labeled them as *"workers of lawlessness."* In spite of their outward appearance of righteousness through indisputably righteous kinds of actions and words, these false practitioners had never been in fellowship with God. Their's was an empty self-confidence.

Jesus explained the simple reason for this complete disconnect: only *"the one who does the will of my Father who is in heaven... will enter the kingdom of heaven" (7:21)*. Even though these individuals used the right words in calling Him *"Lord,"* performed activities known to be associated with Him, and attributed their success to the use of His name the Master clearly indicated they were not doing the will of His Father. For this reason they had no fellowship with Jesus or the Father, in spite of the sincerity of their claims.

What was the basis for this contradictory situation? How could they perform these deeds of righteousness in the name of Jesus while calling Him *"Lord"* and yet, at the same time, not be doing the will of the Father? What key characteristic was missing in their lives that resulted in their disobedience?

Considering the entire context of the Sermon on the Mount, we conclude Jesus was alerting those who would be His followers to the real possibility that they also could become false practitioners by duplicating the failure of their own religious leaders which He had been addressing throughout His entire message...a failure to experience the internal righteousness which gives meaning to external righteousness. Potentially, Jesus' followers could practice a righteousness that did not surpass the righteousness of the Pharisees and teachers of the Law *(5:20)* by living a religion that went no deeper than their outward deeds….and in so doing create their own empty self-confidence.

The Lord was saying to us who would consider ourselves to be kingdom people in today's world, "Be careful! Like the religious leaders of New Testament times, you can become so focused on saying precisely the right words and performing exactly the right actions you will ignore the one thing that validates it all...your inner, spiritual connection with the Father. Be warned! Sincere confidence in the correctness of your words and deeds while you neglect the most important matter, your personal relationship with God, will leave you standing on a foundation of false security. Remember the issue is not that you think you know me; the issue is, do I know you. That is based solely on doing '*the will of the Father' (7:21; Galatians 4:9: 1 Corinthians 8:3; John 14:15, 23-24).*"

Jesus' words plainly remind us that God's will includes not only doing the right actions in the right way, but also supporting those actions with the right spirit, the right motivation, and the right kind of love for the Father. Without that, the Lord warns those of us who with great self-confidence falsely claim to be God's servants, He will never fellowship with us, and, as false practitioners, we will be considered "*workers of lawlessness.*"

CHAPTER 42

7:24-27 ... Build Wisely

"Everyone then who hears these words of mine and does them will be like a wise man who built his house on the rock. And the rain fell, and the floods came, and the winds blew and beat on that house, but it did not fall, because it had been founded on the rock. And everyone who hears these words of mine and does not do them will be like a foolish man who built his house on the sand. And the rain fell, and the floods came, and the winds blew and beat against that house, and it fell, and great was the fall of it."

Throughout the Sermon on the Mount Jesus addressed a variety of life-style issues, sometimes using the power of contrast to drive home His message; for example, a life portraying outward signs of righteousness versus a truly righteous life built on genuine inner dedication to the Lord. While making His points the Master also sprinkled throughout His teaching a variety of attention-getting and sometimes dramatic illustrations. To close the Sermon on the Mount

Jesus used both of these methods in presenting a final word-picture designed to convert the crowd from hearers into doers.

Relying both on the impact of contrast and a dramatic illustration, Jesus explained to His listeners the difference between those who would enjoy great blessing from His teaching and those who would experience failure. The former would become successful kingdom people by duplicating the practices of wise builders. The latter would fail by following the example of foolish builders.

Jesus indicated the successful builder in the kingdom of God, as in any construction project, will begin by selecting a solid foundation. That disciple, He said, will build *"on the rock" (7:24)*, meaning solid bedrock. It is not surprising that Jesus equated *"these words of mine" (7:24)* with rock because at a later time He described Himself as being, *"The stone that the builders rejected" (Matthew 21:42)*. Peter quoted *(1 Peter 2:4-8)* this same Old Testament text *(Psalm 118:22)* and added two others *(Isaiah 28:16; 53:9)* when he also spoke of the Master as being *"the living Stone." [NIV]* Clearly, anyone desiring a productive Christian life must begin by building on the solid rock foundation of Jesus Christ and His teaching.

This same illustration, as given in Luke's writing *(Luke 6:46-49)*, included an additional description of the wise builder. He is one *"who dug deep"* in contrast to the one who simply *"built...on the ground without a foundation."* Wise kingdom builders cannot be satisfied with shallowness and superficiality.

The Holy Spirit produces growth in the soul of the Christian who willingly contributes meaningful and dedicated spiritual sweat equity. Applying Jesus' Sermon on the Mount teaching requires intense self-examination, soul-shaking repentance, and life-altering commitment. The Lord's message reveals to His followers the need for diligent digging through ego, pride, self-interest and stubborn worldly attitudes in order to reach the bedrock foundation required for a strong kingdom building. Such digging requires the straining of one's spiritual muscles and may produce many spiritual backaches, but leads to the foundation for an unshakeable spiritual structure. This *"well built" (Luke 6:48)* house, located on the strongest of foundations, is the product of hearing the words of Jesus and putting them into practice *(7:24)*.

Unfortunately, many people only hear *"these words of (Jesus)" (7:24, 26)*, failing to apply His instruction in their life-building process. James warned strongly against this: *"Do not merely listen to the word, and so deceive yourselves. Do what it says" (James 1:22) [NIV]*. Often people who listen to the same words over and over convince themselves subconsciously that they are doing what they hear. Such self-deception results in false security.

Doing what Jesus said in the Sermon on the Mount can be applied in two ways. The first option focuses on the variety of individual issues the Master addressed - murder/hate, forgiveness/unforgiveness, worry/trust, giving/praying/fasting - and seeks to apply the truths Jesus delivered in regard to each of these matters.

The second option sees the general truth of the entire message that undergirded the individual actions. Time and again the Master confronted His hearers with the problem of performing proper and acceptable deeds, but not supporting them with a pure heart of sincere and righteous dedication to the Lord. Builders guilty of this omission live without the blessing and support of the heavenly Father. Therefore, when the storms of life begin beating on that structure it will fail, falling with a great crash *(7:27)*.

It is important to note that in spite of the distinct contrast between the ending experienced by the foolish builder and that of *"a wise man who built his house on the rock" (7:24)* they both had the same beginning. Jesus described both individuals as being people *"who hear these words of mine" (7:24, 26)*. The difference? One builder, after hearing the Master's words, *"does them" (7:24)*, the other does not *(7:26)*.

With this conclusion to His Sermon on the Mount I, like all people who have listened to the Sermon on the Mount, face some piercing questions: "Am I satisfied with simply hearing Jesus' words or am I also practicing what the Master taught? Does my righteousness surpass the righteousness of the Pharisees and teachers of the law or am I, like them, so focused on outward actions that I neglect the inner purity? Am I building on the right foundation? Will my life-structure stand strong through the storms? Have I anchored myself firmly on the rock-solid foundation...Jesus Christ?"

THE FINAL AUTHORITY FOR THE PRODUCTIVE CHRISTIAN
7:28-29

CHAPTER 43

7:28-29 ... Acknowledge the Supreme Authority

"And when Jesus finished these sayings, the crowds were astonished at his teaching, for he was teaching as one who had authority, and not as their scribes."

Over the past forty-two chapters we have examined the Sermon on the Mount, learning how to walk the path to productive Christian living. In studying Jesus' handbook for Christian living we have discovered He wants us to clothe ourselves in the Beatitudes, but we were informed this would result in persecution *(5:1-12)*. However, He also revealed to us that as Beatitude-clothed servants we would, like *"salt"* and *"light,"* impact the world through our *"good works,"* leading some people to *"give glory to [our] Father in heaven" (5:13-16)*.

Having made clear His own purpose was to fulfill the Law of God *(5:17-19)*, the Lord informed us *"that unless [our] own righteousness exceeds that of the scribes and Pharisees"* we will *"never enter the kingdom of heaven" (5:20)*.

The Master Teacher proceeded next to address the major weakness in the religious activities of the Pharisees of His day. He described their legalistic 'do it precisely the right way' approach which ignored concern for the attitudes of the heart. Using this illustration, the Lord clearly, and sometimes dramatically, emphasized to us the necessity of undergirding one's actions with the right attitudes in personal relationships, inner purity, marital loyalty, personal integrity, and reactions to offenses *(5:21-42)*. He also revealed the single attitude that would produce in our hearts as kingdom people all the other righteous attitudes and make us like our heavenly Father...love *(5:43-47)*.

Jesus then presented three religious activities - giving, prayer, fasting - to show how even we as followers of the Master could be guilty of the same self-centeredness displayed by the Pharisees and teachers of the Law *(6:1-18)*. Through this warning the Lord alerted Christians to the possibility of being caught by the temptation of focusing all our attention on *"practicing [our] righteousness before other people" (6:1)* while ignoring the attitudes giving meaning to those actions. The Master explained our deeds could only be acceptable to the Father if we undergirded them with pure and righteous motivation. Only then would we have a righteousness surpassing that of the Pharisees and teachers of the law.

The Lord also challenged us to establish an objective that would be in sharp contrast to the goal motivating people of the world, who seek primarily to store up earthly treasures. He helped us understand that we will experience productive Christian living by focusing on a different purpose...storing up *"treasures in heaven" (6:20)*. Why? That objective Jesus indicated, would keep us headed the right direction. He assured us, *"where your treasure is, there your heart will be also" (6:19-21)*.

Three practices described by Jesus would help kingdom people keep their hearts in the right place: focus attention in the right place...the light of God *(6:22-23)*; center life's activity in the right place...serving God *(6:24)*; anchor trust in the right place...the faithful heavenly Father *(6:25-34)*. All these can be accomplished by obeying His instruction to establish the right priority... *"Seek first the kingdom of God and his righteousness" (6:33)*.

Christians who travel the path described by Jesus face a dangerous trap along the way. Our continued focus on living a righteous lifestyle can lead us as spiritual travelers to become judgmental toward others who, seemingly, aren't taking the right steps. The Master puts those of us who walk into that trap in the same category as the self-righteous Pharisees... *"You hypocrite" (7:5)*. To be such a hypocritical disciple comes dangerously close to trampling under foot the precious jewels the Lord has offered *(7:6)*.

At this point in Jesus' message we could sincerely feel overwhelmed, and declare, "This kingdom lifestyle is a challenge beyond my ability to fulfill." The Master Teacher assured every doubting disciple that help is available. He assured us the Father in heaven Who is unwavering in faithfulness to His children will respond to our cries for His assistance *(7:7-8)*. In fact, according to the Lord, we can count on the heavenly Father even more than our own earthly fathers *(7:9-11)*. Therefore, as kingdom people we should seek confidently to fulfill the Lord's teaching which He succinctly summarized, *"whatever you wish that others would do to you, do also to them" (7:12)*.

Jesus ended His Sermon on the Mount with two timely warnings and a promise. His warnings caution us to avoid the large crowd of people who choose the wrong road *(7:13-14)* and to be on the watch for false teachers who infiltrate the kingdom crowd *(7:15-23)*. The Master Teacher promised a blessing for disciples who build on the right foundation…Himself and His word. In so doing we are assured we will stand strong throughout all the storms of life *(7:24-27).*

The listeners' reaction to Jesus' mountain-top teaching was unique, completely unlike their response to other teachers. Those hearers were astounded at the Lord's instruction which differed dramatically from what they usually heard. While their own instructors tried to speak authoritatively the people recognized this Teacher actually had authority. Long before Jesus declared, *"All authority in heaven and on earth has been given to me" (Matthew 28:18),* the crowds sensed it and they *"were astonished" (7:28-29).*

Multitudes of hearers over the centuries have evaluated the Sermon on the Mount, the rest of Jesus' teaching, and His entire life. They, like first century believers, recognized that He has all authority because *"Jesus Christ is Lord, to the glory of God the Father" (Philippians 2:11).* Therefore, submitting to His authority, these believers made the Lord Jesus Christ the Master of their lives. Becoming citizens of His kingdom they have chosen to walk the path to productive Christian living. Have you?